Praise for *Inside the* ...

"The *Inside the Minds* series is a valuable probe into the thought, perspectives, and techniques of accomplis' ... Chuck Birenbaum, Partner, Thelen Reid & Pri...

"Unlike any other business ... Debevoise & Plimpton

"A must-read for anyone in the industry." - Dr. Chuck Lucier, Chief Growth Officer, Booz-Allen & Hamilton

"A snapshot of everything you need..." - Charles Koob, Co-Head of Litigation Department, Simpson Thacher & Bartlet

"A great way to see across the changing marketing landscape at a time of significant innovation." - David Kenny, Chairman and CEO, Digitas

"An incredible resource of information to help you develop outside the box..." - Rich Jernstedt, CEO, Golin/Harris International

"Tremendous insights..." - James Quinn, Litigation Chair, Weil Gotshal & Manges

"Great information for both novices and experts." - Patrick Ennis, Partner, ARCH Venture Partners

"A rare peek behind the curtains and into the minds of the industry's best" - Brandon Baum, Partner, Cooley Godward

"Unique insights into the way the experts think and the lessons they've learned from experience." - MT Rainey, Co-CEO, Young & Rubicam/Rainey Kelly Campbell Roalfe

"Intensely personal, practical advice from seasoned dealmakers." - Mary Ann Jorgenson, Coordinator of Business Practice Area, Squire, Sanders & Dempsey

"Great practical advice and thoughtful insights." - Mark Gruhin, Partner, Schmeltzer, Aptaker & Shepard, P.C.

www.Aspatore.com

Aspatore Books is the largest and most exclusive publisher of C-level executives (CEO, CFO, CTO, CMO, partner) from the world's most respected companies. Aspatore annually publishes C-level executives from over half the Global 500, top 250 professional services firms, law firms (managing partners/chairs), and other leading companies of all sizes. By focusing on publishing only C-level executives, Aspatore provides professionals of all levels with proven business intelligence from industry insiders, rather than relying on the knowledge of unknown authors and analysts. Aspatore Books is committed to publishing a highly innovative line of business books, redefining and expanding the meaning of such books as indispensable resources for professionals of all levels. In addition to individual best-selling business titles, Aspatore Books publishes the following unique lines of business books: Inside the Minds, Business Bibles, Bigwig Briefs, C-Level Business Review (Quarterly), Book Binders, ExecRecs, and The C-Level Test, innovative resources for all professionals. Aspatore is a privately held company headquartered in Boston, Massachusetts, with employees around the world.

Inside the Minds

The critically acclaimed *Inside the Minds* series provides readers of all levels with proven business intelligence from C-level executives (CEO, CFO, CTO, CMO, partner) from the world's most respected companies. Each chapter is comparable to a white paper or essay, and is a future-oriented look at where an industry/profession/topic is heading and the most important issues for future success. Each author has been carefully chosen through an exhaustive selection process by the *Inside the Minds* editorial board to write a chapter for this book. *Inside the Minds* was conceived in order to give readers actual insights into the leading minds of business executives worldwide. Because so few books or other publications are actually written by executives in industry, *Inside the Minds* presents an unprecedented look at various industries and professions never before available.

International Advertising

Successful Advertising Techniques from Agencies around the Globe

165101

BOOK IDEA SUBMISSIONS

If you are a C-level executive or senior lawyer interested in submitting a book idea or manuscript to the Aspatore editorial board, please e-mail authors@aspatore.com. Aspatore is especially looking for highly specific book ideas that would have a direct financial impact on behalf of a reader. Completed books can range from 20 to 2,000 pages–the topic and "need to read" aspect of the material are most important, not the length. Include your book idea, biography, and any additional pertinent information.

SPEAKER SUBMISSIONS FOR CONFERENCES

If you are interested in giving a speech for an upcoming ReedLogic conference (a partner of Aspatore Books), please e-mail the ReedLogic Speaker Board at speakers@reedlogic.com. If selected, speeches are given over the phone and recorded (no travel necessary). Due to the busy schedules and travel implications for executives, ReedLogic produces each conference on CD-ROM, then distributes the conference to bookstores and executives who register for the conference. The finished CD-ROM includes the speaker's picture with the audio of the speech playing in the background, similar to a radio address played on television.

INTERACTIVE SOFTWARE SUBMISSIONS

If you have an idea for an interactive business or software legal program, please e-mail software@reedlogic.com. ReedLogic is specifically seeking Excel spreadsheet models and PowerPoint presentations that help business professionals and lawyers accomplish specific tasks. If idea or program is accepted, product is distributed to bookstores nationwide.

Published by Aspatore Inc.

For corrections, company/title updates, comments, or any other inquiries, please e-mail store@aspatore.com.

First Printing, 2005
10 9 8 7 6 5 4 3 2 1

ISBN 1-58762-253-X
Library of Congress Control Number: 2005934876

International Advertising Edited by Michaela Falls, Proofread by Eddie Fournier

Material in this book is for educational purposes only. This book is sold with the understanding that neither any of the authors nor the publisher is engaged in rendering legal, accounting, investment, or any other professional service. Neither the publisher nor the authors assume any liability for any errors or omissions, or for how this book or its contents are used or interpreted, or for any consequences resulting directly or indirectly from the use of this book. For legal advice, please consult your personal lawyer.

The views expressed by the individuals in this book (or the individuals on the cover) do not necessarily reflect the views shared by the companies they are employed by (or the companies mentioned in this book). The employment status and affiliations of authors with the companies referenced are subject to change.

International Advertising

*Successful Advertising Techniques from
Agencies around the Globe*

CONTENTS

Introduction: Advertising at the Speed of Smart

Jordan Zimmerman
Chief Executive Officer and Chairman
Zimmerman & Partners Advertising
United States

Succeeding in Advertising

Show me a successful client, and I'll show you a successful agency. Success in advertising is connected ultimately to the success of the client. At Zimmerman & Partners Advertising, we embrace that principle. To be successful, you must be involved. You must take the time to learn your client's business and brand attributes well. Let the client know that you care as much about the business as he or she does. Analyze the business, its chief competitors, its unique culture, mission, vision, and trends of the category it's in. Most importantly, stay focused on brand attributes upon which the client can build. Be single-minded. Literally. Don't throw many attributes out there in the hope they'll take away just one. Be certain *the one* is the one you want them to take away. If you don't know your client's business intimately, you are likely to focus on attributes that really aren't important to the consumer, often at the client's request. It's your uncomfortable obligation to be honest and say, "That's an attribute that has no meaning to the consumer." Recommend what is right for the business, what is supported by logic, research, and solid, strategic thinking; that which differentiates your brand from the competition. Only then can you communicate in a compelling manner. Only then can you cut through the clutter and attract the interest and attention the client needs to grow its business. For more than twenty-five years, this has been my strategy for success.

Five Not-so-Easy Pieces for Success

There are five essential skill sets in advertising. The first is accountability. The bar is set with the client's business objectives. Then we raise it a few notches higher. Our philosophy is that image-building and branding must always be balanced against the need to deliver on the bottom line. Advertising is a means to an end, not an end in itself. Successful clients make the best clients; we want to create brand leaders—clients with skyrocketing sales and sparkling creative.

The second essential skill is media savvy. With media fragmentation increasing exponentially, each medium must be understood for what it is really capable of delivering. It must be targeted precisely and assessed with the end user in mind. As with creative, media planning and placement must build the client's business.

The third essential skill is unyielding commitment. You are more than the agency; you must be an evangelist, preaching the virtues of your client to your staff, your client's staff, and the public. We must be committed advocates, as well as dedicated business partners. The entrepreneurial approach we apply to each of our clients' businesses must be evident in every phase of the advertising development, from planning to creative to execution. No task is too big and, equally important, no job is too small. It is also crucial to be proactive. It is essential to deliver more than what the client asks for.

The fourth essential skill is to be disciplined. At our firm, we assist clients in focusing on the compelling, differentiating selling points that induce consumer consideration. We must never lose sight of that focus as we move from creative development through media planning and execution. We seek to reach targeted consumers with an effective, focused communication to which they will respond. Say one thing. Say it well. Say it often.

The fifth essential skill is creativity, the art of being inventive and imaginative. We must apply creativity to everything we do—tirelessly exploring innovative ways to communicate the brand selling point in a meaningful, relevant way. A message has to break through and resonate with the consumer to be successful. Consumers are not waiting for your message. You must deliver it to them in an unexpected manner. Creative has an aftershock. It will be felt long after it stops running. When that happens, you've done your job. That's creativity you can't put a price on.

Advertising and Branding

Advertising allows you to communicate a salient message to a large group of consumers faster than any other form of communication. It allows you to truly connect with the consumer; it gives you an opportunity to develop an ongoing relationship between the consumer and a brand. At its best, advertising will create a sense of urgency for the consumer, an awareness—often honest and accurate—that there are products, places, styles, or sensibilities that cry out for action or attention.

Breakthrough ideas might appear to be instant or impulsive, but they are not. They are based on sound strategy, outstanding visuals and copy, and the correct application of timing and media. The art is in ensuring that all elements of communication work together so that the end result is more powerful and effective. It's like conducting a symphony orchestra—all the instruments working together, the timing just right to make beautiful music. In the world of advertising, this is a total business solution. We don't see ourselves as an "advertising" agency. We're the conductors helping to orchestrate a business success.

There are various styles of advertising—a soft sell or a hard sell, a subtle approach or a blatant approach, an informative style or a modern and edgy one. Style will always change: with the product or service you are selling, with the timing of the message, with the medium you are using. Style will also be influenced by the life stage of the brand. You can use different styles of advertising with a mature brand like Coca-Cola, more than you can with a new brand or one that is declining or has lost its way. The important thing is finding the right balance between defining a brand and delivering next-day sales. The true craft is in identifying ways to interest consumers in what is being offered. A creative strategy can put you on the right course, but in a world filled with clutter and distractions you must develop communications that capture consumer attention and interest. The key is delivering the selling point in an interesting, single-minded, non-contrived manner. Some advertising sells brands. Great advertising also builds them.

Assuming a client's product or service meets an immediate or unfulfilled future need, it must deliver on three or four attributes differentiating it from whatever else is out there. Let's take our client Nissan as an example. Nissan sells a basic commodity: cars. However, Nissan not only delivers exceptional value, it understands how to differentiate itself from the competition, employing persuasive messaging that hits at the core audience's relevant needs. However, there is another level of understanding here: Nissan is smart about building cars because it understands through relevant research what potential customers need and what they want. It's our job to identify those core attributes—match them with consumer desire and bring them to life in our advertising and marketing campaigns. As a result, during the consumer's consideration process, Nissan ranks high on the shopping list. We know what triggers a consumer's desire beyond price point alone. We don't want to get caught up in a price game; like Nissan, we must be strategically smarter than that by promoting exceptional quality at affordable prices—advertising to both the heart and the mind.

Once a brand's core attributes are defined, the message must be communicated to generate customer awareness—a message that incorporates the basic tenets of the brand promise: quality, price, customer service, and follow-up. This must all be done on a consistent basis with the long term in mind. Great brands are not fads. A great brand is just that—a brand that understands how to differentiate itself and become a consumer presence.

Today, discipline in advertising is vitally important because of the intensely competitive environment and the need for immediate results. Discipline means being true to a brand's strategy and staying focused. Too often, we see advertising that is so off strategically that it does irreparable harm to a brand. Often, this happens because a concept perceived as "exciting" or "breakthrough" is actually confusing, unfocused, and lacking in clarity. The brand loses its way and its potential customers because of a lack of discipline. We believe that if we understand and define what a brand stands for, who the consumers are, and what key attributes they are seeking, we will always be on strategy.

Of course, for a brand to break through, it must meet a valid, relevant consumer need. The message then must be focused and single-minded, so that the consumer takeaway is clear and distinct. Second, there must be enough of the right message delivered to the right target audience in the right medium to be remembered. The product or service must deliver on the promise.

Great brands have the ability to manifest themselves through different styles and different copy points, as long as the brand's core message is consistent. In a highly fragmented market with highly targeted media—specialty publications, cable television, or specific-format radio stations—we can deliver different styles of messaging to the marketplace and lessen the risk of sending a mixed message. The trouble starts when the product does not deliver on the attributes communicated or when the attributes are far removed from how the product is perceived in the marketplace. At our firm, we never sacrifice clarity for the sake of style or execution.

However, it's our experience that the core component of the brand message must contain some specific, consistent elements. For example, we have been instrumental in helping one of our clients, Lennar Homes, build on its concept called EI—Everything's Included. Consumers are often frustrated walking into new homes that are absolutely gorgeous, deciding to buy one, and then discovering that everything in the model is an expensive upgrade. Our idea with Lennar Homes was to give them a point of differentiation: When you walk into the model, what you see is what you get. It's affordable. Wall Street loved the idea, and analysts said EI was one of the most successful concepts in the housing category. Customers walk into a Lennar home and everything's included, but they also receive top-quality merchandise instead of having to upgrade it themselves, incurring that incremental cost. The house might be a little more expensive, but ultimately the customer is getting more value. This has proven quite successful for Lennar Homes: They're a leading homebuilder in the United States today and a Wall Street darling. Their stock has continued to grow, even in these risky times. It's all due to differentiating themselves with a concept that reaches consumers in their hearts, their minds, and, most importantly, their pockets—a "value" story that was most valuable to Lennar.

In my opinion, it is significantly harder to achieve this kind of breakthrough today. Sectors are busier, and substitutes and competitors can come to market faster today than in the past—so fast, it's almost scary. The proliferation of media options requires a smarter approach today than it did just a few years ago. Think about it: We used to have three networks—ABC, CBS, and NBC. Today the range of options, given cable and satellite television, is unbelievable. There used to be a few key publications, radio, and no online media. Today everything is coming at you. In the wrong hands, multimedia can dilute a message. In the right hands, you can hammer it home.

Growing or Killing a Brand

It is important to understand the lifecycle of a category, a brand, and a product to take a brand to the next level and drive long-term success. New brands must establish a niche. A mature brand must find new life, possibly by reinventing itself through extensions or by creating a new identity that connects with today's consumers. Finding more core customers or finding new customers for the brand are challenges that require different approaches. Building on your strengths with customers who truly like and need your product is easier than developing a new customer group. It is mandatory to constantly refresh your consumer data and research to keep up with the trends. Things are moving faster today than ever before; consumers are smarter than ever.

While finding new customer segments, there is always the challenge of not offending current customers while building the brand with the new target group that may have different core needs and require a different advertising approach. For example, Oldsmobile had a longtime hold on its market segment. The market inevitably became older and older. At that time, Oldsmobile decided to run a "This is not your father's Oldsmobile" campaign. What happened? Not only did it not attract a new audience, it turned off its core audience. The result: Oldsmobile declined as a brand.

We have a handful of brands around today that will stand the test of time. Coca-Cola is one. Ford might be another, but it will take some luck, some very smart brand and business management, and no crisis situations. Who would have thought Arthur Andersen would disappear? Who could have foreseen the Goodyear tire fiasco with the Ford Explorer? Brands must be nimble; their stewards must know how to evolve and have the commitment to make the changes necessary to continue to be great. It is important to react quickly, but you must move at the "speed of smart."

Typically, what kills an established brand is bad management, lack of foresight and vision—stewards who have become complacent and don't take risks or have allowed the product to lose its connection to the consumer. Bad product, marketing, or pricing decisions can kill a brand over time. Environmental and ethical issues can kill a brand overnight. A discontinuity will kill a brand today. No one knows what unfulfilled need is around the corner that will allow consumers to substitute one product for another. Tic Tacs appeared and eroded Dentyne's market share overnight. Dentyne never saw it coming.

If some of a brand's core attributes have become less relevant to today's consumer, then a brand will have to reinvent itself to survive and grow. It is usually a tougher challenge to invent a new brand completely. If a brand has a strong but eroding foundation, it has a base to build on. Evolving a brand doesn't necessarily mean a complete reinvention. Budweiser is a good example of a brand staying fresh in its approach without constantly reinventing itself.

Advertising Pitfalls

There are four main pitfalls in advertising. The first is strategic: a lack of strategic foundation and focus, a mismatch of target and product, a bland, vanilla positioning platform, a lack of differentiation, and a lack of relevance. It's just like life: It's good to know what you want to say before you open your mouth.

There are creative pitfalls. These include trying to communicate too many attributes that mean little to the consumer, which, in a sense, is a strategic shortcoming. There's playing it safe. Safe is not what makes great brands. Safe is not what inspires consumers to buy great brands. Safe is not where we as advertising agencies want to be. Safe won't change anything. There's lack of style, interest, and the hard-to-define ability to cut through clutter. If you don't have style in your advertising, it isn't interesting, it can't cut through clutter, and you are wasting your client's dollar. Your client, by the way, should look for a new agency.

Third, there are media pitfalls—especially spending too thinly. We talk a lot about frequency. We are hit with thousands of different messages every day. How can we respond? Frequency is the future of advertising and marketing. Spreading yourself too thinly prevents you from having the kind of frequency you need to drive sales. It's inefficient spending. Media that whispers isn't heard. If you don't have many dollars to spend, don't spread them too thinly. Instead, spend in appropriate channels. If we're not effective in our targeting, we won't be effective in delivering the results for the client. The most creative, compelling message is useless if nobody is hearing or seeing it.

Finally, there are measurement pitfalls: measurement tools are not in place, realistic yet achievable goals are not set, an audit is not completed. You have to know what's working and what's not working. At our firm, we have designed proprietary programs such as Ztrac, a real-time, Internet-based platform that tracks traditional medias and enables us to monitor our client's progress. Ultimately, successful advertising is like a journey: You need a map to arrive at a destination, and you need markers warning of detours and impassable roads. Without measurement, there are no markers, nothing to direct you to your destination or warn you of the cliff up ahead. Stay aggressive. There should always be a set goal—but never a finish line.

Budgeting and Return on Investment

We work with large budgets, small ones, and others in the middle. The secret in making a budget work is resource allocation: Focus on those areas that have the greatest efficiencies and effectiveness given the size of the budget you have. If you have the resources, a truly integrated approach allows you to be persuasive with the message and to hit your target customers whomever, whenever, and wherever they may be. You can spend money on extensive research and preparing to deliver your message. You can put the right systems and processes in place to effectively track and measure the advertising. You can set a true customer relationship management program in place and have the time to get it right through testing and refinement. Having the ability to use interactive media allows you to be ahead of the curve before your competitors have a chance to either understand or test these approaches themselves. I believe that if you have the time and the money, anything can be accomplished because you can lead yourself strategically from the beginning to the end with very little risk. But always remember, having all the money in the world and simply throwing it at a problem will not solve it—you still have to aim.

If spending is a factor, radio is an extremely effective tool. The key with smaller budgets is to focus, prioritize, and not try to do too much. All too often we see clients with very small budgets who want to compete against companies with much larger market share. Copycatting is not an effective tactic for penetrating a market, particularly with a small budget. Often, however, you can break through using radio, a medium that has not been used effectively even by the bigger ad agencies. Radio is highly effective on a cost-per-point basis. Most importantly, it works and is a good responsive medium. Some reasons for this are that drive times in the United States have become longer rather than shorter, and people have become more infatuated with radio/traffic reports/news bulletins than ever before, thus offering a captive audience. Our job is to have an effective communication strategy to break through on the radio.

We measure return on investment through sales, sales, sales. The questions to ask are: Did the cash register ring? Did we deliver sales revenue in an affordable and profitable way? Did we deliver market share? Did we become the talk and the preference? If we did, then we were successful on all fronts.

A successful advertising campaign accomplishes the stated objectives and beats them. Objectives are set, measurement parameters are defined, and a campaign is developed, launched, and measured accordingly. Intuitively, a successful campaign is one that effectively reaches target audiences in a memorable, compelling way and motivates them to act with immediacy. We don't have time to wait for them to act. What we do must inspire them to act now. We must hit at the heartstrings (i.e., forge an emotional connection) with the products we're moving. Advertising is not entertainment; it is a sales tool.

The old adage of whether the cup is half full or half empty no longer holds in today's business climate. Our clients are demanding—their advertising must work, and it must work now. They don't have the time or the marketing dollars to waste waiting for a marketing message to sink in and then wait even longer for it to eventually drive sales. It is all about accountability, more so than ever before in our industry. Therefore, advertising today is more fun, more challenging, and at the same time we see our results enhance our own bottom line.

Ultimately, it all comes back to the client. We always have to keep the best interests of the client in mind. It isn't about the agency. It isn't about winning awards. It's about our client's business. They hired us as an advertising agency to do one thing: to help their business, to grow their brand strategically. So we need to learn to manage their budgets and spend their money like it is our own. Then we need to measure results, as much as we monitor our own return on investment. If we are not achieving the results, we need to learn why and not make that same mistake again. The bottom line is that it all comes down to their bottom line, period.

The necessity of accountability will continue to strengthen until it becomes top-of-mind for agencies and clients. More and more agencies will have to quantify the impact they are having on their clients' businesses. They will have to illustrate specifically how advertising initiatives are advancing company goals. Simply creating ads will not be enough for agencies to succeed. Agencies will need to go further and develop nontraditional ways to grow clients' businesses. This includes delivering alternative marketing initiatives and providing strategic insight on how clients can grow and run their businesses, be it through line extensions, acquisitions, or distribution channel expansion. Agencies need to show they are valuable business partners that share clients' goals rather than pursue their own goals as agencies. They need to show they are true strategic partners present every step of the way, giving their clients guidance and a view from outside their networks. Smart clients and confident agencies will tie compensation programs directly to results.

Changes in the Industry

Five years ago, many people saw the Internet and technology as the future of selling. What we've learned is that the consumer has used it to be more informed and educated, to make more of a rational decision about the products or services he or she wants to buy. It allows advertisers to interact with end users in the privacy of their homes or offices, and on their own timetables. It allows us to track quickly the dynamics of fast-changing markets and to react on our clients' behalves. It allows us to track and measure the effectiveness of our advertising campaigns in real time.

The Internet will continue to grow and be important in some industries and with some products and brands. Technology will continue to evolve, and we'll use those innovations that make us more productive and effective in what we do. However, using technology just for the sake of being leading-edge is counterproductive as evidenced by the soaring bankruptcies, poor performance, and increasing client resistance to the overstated promise of the Internet and interactive agencies. Like strong creative, technology is a tool, not an end in itself.

Technology is an enabler throughout all stages of the advertising process, from creative development, to the delivery of advertising, to measurement and tracking. Technology has changed the speed and quality of the advertising we deliver. For example, we can now record—in our studios— voice or music talent from around the world to be used in our commercials. At our firm, we house our own studios so we can do it better, faster, and more affordably for our clients. We can record a saxophone player in Los Angeles, voice talent in Detroit, and somebody else in Europe all at the same time with digital quality. It's become part of the dynamic world we live in today. Technology allows us to react, to make changes in our work in a matter of minutes rather than days.

Broadband is a so-called disruptive technology from an advertising perspective (i.e., it will interrupt or dramatically change the way we do things). It is taking some time to gain wide acceptance and achieve critical mass but will become, among other things, the fourth pillar of the media world. It plays a role in advertising on demand. Other upcoming applications of technology include animation and robotics. Animation is not currently at a cost-effective stage and is not realistic enough to use extensively in commercials in place of human talent. Robotics will one day allow us to shoot television commercials in places we could never go, or do things we can only imagine.

In the future, advertising will become even more persuasive, and optional. Consumers will be able to shut out irrelevant or incomprehensible messages. We'll be given more opportunities to accept only messages we want to receive, whether broadcast or online. We will also be able to program the types of ads we want. If we like humorous ads, we'll see only humorous ads. At some future point, the agency will need to target carefully and make sure messages are clear, relevant, and desirable to audiences, knowing they will be able to pick and choose.

In the next five years, advertising will be faster, of higher quality, and more targeted. True one-on-one marketing means a different message communicated to every consumer. We'll move a bit closer to that over the next five years, which means advertising executives will have to stay on top of their game—and everyone else's game—that much more.

Advertising is a fun, but challenging business. Today the consumer wants more and more; that need must be served, as every market sector becomes more competitive. There were four or so brands in the automotive sector in 1956. Today there are more than thirty brands, and the same is true in other sectors. It is extremely difficult to be dominant: You have to be smart to be the best in a splintered market. Clients won't stay for the wrong reasons. The brand is the lifeblood of any corporation. It is up to the adverting agency to grow, defend, and support its promise.

Jordan Zimmerman is chief executive officer and chairman of the board of Zimmerman & Partners Advertising.

At age eight, he started the only greeting card sales route in New Jersey and for the next three years went door-to-door selling "good wishes" and "holiday cheer." He sold the venture at age eleven, turning his first profit.

The next year, he built a newspaper delivery empire that employed other neighborhood kids and expanded operating efficiency and customer satisfaction. The experience taught him that building a successful business is a team sport; you just can't do it alone.

While working with NIDA during his senior year of college, Mr. Zimmerman recognized the true power of words when a girl in a focus group on drug abuse responded with, "I just say no." Consequently, he led the "Just Say No" marketing initiative during the Carter administration (one of the most recognizable anti-drug campaigns to date). He founded Zimmerman & Partners Advertising in 1984.

Today, his advertising agency is one of the largest and most successful in the United States. Coining the phrase "Brandtailing," Mr. Zimmerman effectively merged the elements of branding and retailing to develop an advertising discipline that creates positive long-term brand identity, as well as short-term retail results.

Australia

Peter James Ryan
Head, Retail Strategy Consulting
IdeaWorks

Highlights

Most Common Advertising Methods

- Electronic – television, radio, cinema, Internet
- Print – press, magazine
- Direct marketing
- Catalogue distribution (unsolicited letterbox drops and newspaper inserts)
- Outdoor
- Ambient
- Sponsorship and events
- Viral

How Advertising is Different in Australia

Advertising in Australia is similar to advertising in the United States. It tends to be dominated by free-to-air television channels and is increasingly affected by cable television and Internet erosion of advertising dollar share. Alternative forms of promotion are constantly being explored and are gaining acceptability. Direct marketing is undertaken by certain market segments and, due to differences in mail distribution regulations in Australia, unsolicited catalogues still form part of the promotional distribution of many marketers.

A common mistake made by foreigners is assuming Australia is another state of the United States in terms of style and content. This assumption results in the blind application of international business models or promotional material that is neither behaviorally, culturally, nor geographically appropriate for the Australian market. Australia basically has the population base of New York City and the Burroughs or Greater London spread across a landmass the size of the continental United States. The primary concentration of this population is coastal and increasingly the greater Sydney basin. Australia is also a cultural melting pot and has been for some decades. While the percentage of Hispanic population is lower in Australia than the United States, we have the largest Greek population outside Athens in Melbourne, a large number of first-generation Italians,

Asians, and other ethnicities blended into a historically white Anglo-Saxon English heritage. Australia is a unique place. Founded on the back of a penal colony, our attitude toward authority and political patriotism is cynical, and our natural sense of humor is based on irony. Another mistake is the application of global brand campaigns without introduction and relevance. Brands often overestimate their power when entering this market and assume a sense of saliency or intimacy that is underserved. Australia is not a parochial market, quite the opposite in that it embraces the world and change. However, many brands have forgotten how long it took them to build brand trust in their domestic markets, and hence try to take a fast track approach or—even worse—assume they are in the same position here as they are domestically. Relationships take time, and in Australia we prefer to have a conversation before we jump into bed together.

How News is Dispersed

News is still broken in morning newspapers first, then morning radio, and then reflected in evening television news. If an important story is being covered at length—for example, the Gulf War—CNN, Fox News, or Sky News on cable television becomes a key access point for throughout-the-day updates.

Major News Outlets

Newspapers:
- News Limited
- Fairfax
- APN News and Media
- Rural Press Ltd.

Magazines:
- ACP – Australian Consolidated Press
- Pacific Publications
- Murdoch Magazines
- FPC – Magazines

News wires:
- AAP – Australian Associated Press

Television networks:
- Seven Network (metropolitan)
- Nine Network (metropolitan)
- Ten Network (metropolitan)
- Seven Network affiliates (regional)
- Nine Network affiliates (regional)
- Southern Cross Media Sales (ten regional)
- Foxtel (pay television)
- Optus (pay television)
- SBS
- ABC

Internet:
- Nine MSN
- News Interactive
- F2
- Sensis MediaSmart

Radio:
- austereo
- ARN – Australian Radio Network
- DMG – Daily Mail Group
- RG Capital
- Southern Cross Broadcasting
- Macquarie Network

Advertising Related Resources

We use many reference sites, from WGSN to Forbes.com to National Retailers Federation. We also use domestic marketing publications and international publications such as *Ad Age*, *Ad News*, *B&T*, *Campaign*, *Campaign Brief*, *Retail Week*, the Roy Morgan Database, and so on.

How Advertising Works in Australia

While Australians speak English, we are a different market than the United States and the United Kingdom. Television is still the channel to launch and maintain brand, print media are used for information support and tactical promotion, and radio is used for frequency. Consumption of media is still relatively high on a per capita basis in Australia.

Australian advertising is very much driven by message relevance to the consumer. While divided into tactical promotion (sales getting) and brand building, as it is in most markets, the larger slice falls into the former category. The majority of advertising is for known brands driving sales-getting activity.

In Australia, as everywhere in the world, advertising means knowing where you are—the stage of your relationship with the consumer you are speaking to. If you are in the earliest stages of a relationship, then you are introducing yourself and creating reasons to interact—to grow acceptance and familiarity. Once the relationship is established, advertising is about keeping the relationship fresh and stimulating and capitalizing on it. Later on, it is about reminding the consumer why you are their best choice. Australian consumers—like those in many Western nations—have an overabundance of choice. They seek relevance to them and reasons to buy. As consumers of anything, we are very good at filtering out what we see lacks relevance. "Don't waste my time. I'd rather be at the beach," is a common piece of feedback.

Therefore, creative messages must either entertain or inform consumers (or both), but not waste their time. Increasingly, advertising is seen as something that must engage or risk the powerful editing force of the consumer and competition for attention and comprehension.

In identifying target markets, Australian consumers and audiences are segmented using most contemporary means—Mosaic codes, demographics, household income from census data, age, psychographics, behavioral segmentation, and so on. These types of segmentation are readily available. One of the most common is a data set called Roy Morgan Single Source data. All media and advertising agencies in Australia have access to this data, and it is a common source to use for all the above types of segmentation. The choice of segmentation method used is usually determined by the advertiser.

Advertising Methods and Costs

Subject to budget, television is still the most potent advertising weapon. Direct marketing from a customer relationship management framework is gathering momentum and budget. Many retailers in particular still use letterbox drops of catalogues on a weekly basis for product and price promotion. All other media are used to support or enhance individual campaign objectives.

Advertising costs vary widely, of course, but for a national brand to advertise nationwide, production costs can be as little as AUD$10,000 for a finished television commercial or as much as AUD$2 million. A national television schedule of any note rarely makes an impact below AUD$2 million. Magazine production depends on the creative direction, but can range from AUD$5,000 to AUD$500,000. A national campaign in a major magazine title would range from AUD$15,000 to AUD$75,000 per full page. Newspaper advertising production parallels magazine production, and full-page rates range from AUD$8,000 per full page for regional newspapers to AUD$120,000 for one full page carried in all the metropolitan markets.

Ideaworks' Services

Ideaworks' area of focus is retail. Therefore, we have built a one-stop shop for retailers, with services including everything from retail consulting through store design and architecture, staff training, customer relationship management, advertising, direct marketing, visual merchandising, sales promotion, design, Internet design, and more—whatever a retailer needs to implement a retail marketing strategy. We can offer everything from advice to implementation, tracking, and performance analysis.

All promotional campaigns should have as a goal that they contribute in a meaningful way to sustainable profit growth for the brand. How they should go about doing that can only be established on a case-by-case basis.

IdeaWorks uses a 7P framework (product, pricing, place, people, process, presentation, promotion) to develop implementation plans around a customer value proposition or core competency, rephrased as a competitive advantage. In retail as distinct from packaged or branded goods, consumer touch points are many and varied, with many being far more powerful in terms of residual perception than advertising. For this reason, in retail promotion, the critical difference in approach is that promotion supports the brand rather than leading it. The core competency of the business and the cultural approach of the business are the most important aspects that determine their relationship to customers. Consistent reinforcement of these aspects as expressed through a customer value proposition are the umbrella guides for touch point consistency throughout a complex and extended mix of activities. Promotional activities are seen as a part of this mix. All activity is reviewed within the context of sales performance on a quarterly basis.

Favorite Tools

The greatest challenge we face is establishing differentiation in customers' hearts and minds in what is a saturated space.

For retail, the ultimate promotional tools are a combination of a fully resourced customer relationship management database program and television advertising. This is still the most powerful combination to create brand magnetism at the top and individual customer relevance-of-offer to affect behavior at the bottom.

When there is a very tight budget, we can use the retail space/store and the store staff as the medium.

In Australia, Internet sales are in their infancy—though growing rapidly. However, as an information medium, the Internet is widely used. Most major advertisers now ensure that, at the very least, they use the Internet as a part of their communication with consumers and that they are testing Internet advertising (banner, burst, click-through). We are actively building our customers' e-commerce, brochure ware, and online advertising capabilities.

Best Advice

The best advertising advice I ever received was to always ask two questions: What is the one thing you want the consumer to take from this piece of communication, and, as a result of having seen it, what is it you want them to do next? Since the 1950s, sociologists have proven that our attention spans have physiologically shortened. This has primarily come about as a self-protection mechanism to cope with the increasing bombardment of messages created by the escalating communications revolution. Today, the only chance of cutting through and being remembered is to focus any piece of communication of one message—simple, loud, and clear. What is the one thing you are trying to tell them and what do you want them to do about it? Do you want them to call a telephone number, visit a store, tell a friend, go to the window and shout out...or do nothing?

The advice I most frequently give others is to treat consumers' time with respect. Entertain them, inform them, or—better still—do both. Make sure what you are trying to communicate to them is relevant to them.

Changes and Trends in Advertising

The major development in advertising in the past five to ten years has been the gradual erosion of time spent consuming the main media by the average person. Competition for attention (cut-through) and comprehension is becoming increasingly difficult, and tolerance is dropping rapidly. In most areas of life, consumers have a constant and unquenchable thirst for stimulation. The historical advertising paradigm has been about repetition, and this is diametrically opposed to consumers' need for constant newness and change.

In the future, I see advertising adopting methods that will make it cheaper and easier to create constantly changing stimulus for consumers—stimulus that is relevant to them, informative, entertaining, and memorable, but nonetheless constantly changing and staying fresh.

Influencing the influencers, reaching peer groups, and finding new and different ways to create an introduction are becoming the norm. As natural trust is annihilated, an introduction to the consumer is becoming essential.

A recommendation from someone you trust, an anecdote from a spokesperson, a friend letting you try theirs: these are all ways of gently being introduced to something new. Adoption may be fast after this stage, but getting past this stage is a slow process of earning enough trust to be sampled or tried out.

Special interest media, portable media, and relevant interruption media are all up-and-coming ways of getting to the right people. Product placement in movies, television shows, magazines, books, radio programs, events, and the like are also key influence points for initial contact.

Once a relationship has begun, everything is then about reinforcement of what attracts them to the business/brand in the first place, in a consistent yet stimulating manner.

Peter James Ryan is a strategic marketing consultant with more than twenty-five years of marketing and promotional experience. Having worked in roles as diverse as business management, marketing management, consulting, and creative services through a myriad of categories and businesses, Mr. Ryan has a unique perspective on how to apply marketing thinking to the retail field. Acknowledged as a passionate advocate of the retail industry, his love affair with the category can be traced back to family involvement in the ownership and operation of various retail businesses.

Mr. Ryan's pervious experience includes group general manager of the Banks Group (marketing consulting and research), head of marketing for St. George Bank Group, head of strategy for Lunn Dyer Group, head of strategy and creative for Harrison Holt BBDO, and more recently, head of strategic planning for IdeaWorks. He has been responsible for the development of some of Australia's leading retail initiatives, retail brands, retail customer experiences, retail environments, and retail service initiatives.

Brazil

Eduardo Fischer
Chief Executive Officer and Chairman
Grupo Total de Comunicação

Advertising in Brazil is normally recognized by its daring creative work, by the high level of creativity of its professionals, and for the good-humored appeal that goes along with intelligent ideas.

This is the difference between good Brazilian advertising and good advertising in other countries. Brazilian advertising has managed to stand out in international festivals with high doses of creativity and low production budgets.

Among the most awarded countries in the world, like Japan, England, the United States, and Spain, Brazil is always the poor underdog in the business, the country with the least amount of resources available for production. When Brazilian advertising competes with other countries, this is not taken into account, which only reinforces the importance of the quality of our creative product.

Successful Advertising Strategies in Brazil

Advertisers must be aware that there are enormous cultural, social, and regional differences in a country with the continental dimensions of Brazil. Despite having significant economic problems to face, Brazil has many highly sophisticated and well-informed consumers who know what they want.

To serve this consumer, advertising must be sophisticated as well. It has to contain information that is exactly in tune with what this consumer needs to know. Advertisers shouldn't try elementary advertising or formulas that may work in other countries, because they are not necessarily effective here. Brazilian consumers have their own peculiarities. They are educated consumers who value consumption and make the best use of their money because, on average, this consumer does not have an elevated purchasing power. So it is always important to observe these characteristics.

Let me give you a good example of this by quoting a statement that became famous, which was made by Joazinho Trinta, a carnival designer: "In Brazil, poor people like luxury. Poverty is for the intellectuals."

The biggest mistake made by foreigners who advertise in Brazil is the globalization of their ideas. Large companies come here and use the same ideas adopted for Mexico, the United States, and France. This doesn't work. Readymade campaigns produced abroad and simply translated to the local language don't usually succeed, save for a few rare exceptions. One of the few exceptions is McDonald's, which adapted a global campaign to the Brazilian culture with extraordinary success, and helped boost the image of the chain in the country.

Reaching the Masses

News is normally communicated through printed or electronic media. Television and radio are the most comprehensive media, but printed media is extremely relevant at a regional level. Currently, Brazil prints 2,993 newspapers, 529 of which are daily newspapers and directed toward different reader profiles. The Brazilian magazine market is composed of 1,582 titles in fifty-six different categories. There are three different publications of general interest that reach more than 8 million readers weekly.

There are many Brazils within Brazil. It has regions that resemble India, others that resemble Bulgaria, and others that resemble Belgium, in terms of behavior and consumption standards. Consequently, it is useless trying to talk to the Brazilian population as a whole. Understanding the regional differences and taking advantage of them is instrumental. In this context, the greatest challenge for advertising is to stimulate consumption without disrespecting those consumers who wish to buy but do not have a sufficient level of income.

Segmentation of targets in Brazil is done by gender, age, and social class, with multiple combinations. The social and economic classification considers the level of education of the head of the family and the possession of certain items of consumption of the household, generating a final score that determines the social class for the specific home. This criterion, known as "criterion Brazil," is adopted by the major survey institutes that measure ratings and consumptions of the communication media.

Measuring Success

We are strategic partners to our clients. We are more than an advertising agency. We act as a true consultancy, whose prime activity is to understand our clients' business, and then we draw a plan for integrated communications that has a great concept as a starting point. This concept is generated by our profound understanding of our clients' business, as well as the behavior and needs of consumers.

Our performance is characterized by a practice we call Total Communication (Comunicação Total®, a registered trademark for the company in sixteen countries throughout Latin America). This work methodology integrates, under one concept, the various communication tools, seeking greater synergy, and above all, the best result for our clients: advertising, no media/below-the-line communication, promotional marketing, incentive marketing, relationship marketing, loyalty promotional programs, direct marketing, promotions, incentive campaigns directed to middle audiences, and so on.

Our measure of success is meeting the goals established by our clients. For example, when the Grupo Schincariol[1] began working with Fischer, their annual sales totaled R$900 million per year. After one year, the beverage company had hiked its sales to R$1.74 billion, a result much higher than expected by the company, credited to the extraordinary success of the Comunicação Total® campaign, which we created for their major product, the *Nova Schin* beer.

The case "Nova Schin"—which conquered the Silver Medal in the AME International Awards for 2005 in the "Best Use of Discipline in the Integrated Marketing" category—presents a planned and implemented strategy for repositioning the product in the market. An appropriate and original use of marketing tools enabled the brand to triumph in an extraordinarily competitive segment through an optimum use of media, promotion, endomarketing, and public relations. Success brought New

---

[1] The Grupo Schincariol is a beverage company that produces beer, soft drinks, bottled water, and juices. Established in 1939, it is one of Brazil's largest soft drink manufacturers and is among the 500 largest companies in Brazil; it has 6,000 direct employees. Its 2004 annual sales were of the order of R$2.54 billion.

Schin a real growth in sales and brand recall. In 2004, the company—thanks to the success of the Nova Schin campaign—had a Lajida profit 230 percent greater than in 2003.

Advertising is always about sales. It's meeting our clients' goals and surprising them with exceptional results.

The campaign of my dreams is to sell Brazil by improving the image of the country abroad. I would make a large campaign using all the tools available in the Comunicação Total® to change the perception that Brazil is only a country of samba, carnival, and soccer. I would create a vast calendar of actions, promotions, events, trade shows, and publicity campaigns to show Brazil exactly the way it really is.

When you have a tight budget, a good idea makes the difference. Often, the simplest idea is the best. I recall a memorable commercial made for Seagram Company Ltd. that showed a boy smiling in slow motion. This image was identified with the brand, the concept that the company manufactured wonderful products, but that the most important thing was to respect limits, because life was made up of other things. This was a spectacular idea, with a low budget.

Another extremely simple and low-cost commercial was for Coca-Cola, and it used bottle caps and containers to say the soft drink was for everyone—the weak, the overweight, and the thin. It was a sensational commercial made only about the product.

We produced a great commercial for a manufacturer of distilled liquor, Tatuzinho, which received the Silver Lion in the Cannes festival. To communicate new product packaging in PET bottles (plastic package), we showed a woman singing opera in a high pitch that broke everything around her, except for the bottle of Tatuzinho. This was another simple idea, easily executed, that had a large impact.

Capitalizing on the Internet

Brazil ranks eighth in the number of Web surfers (20.6 million), with 12.2 million active users (accessing more than one week per month). The categories most visited are the portals and search sites, which cover an average 85.6 percent of active Web surfers, representing 10.5 million unique visitors per month.

There was a great evolution in the last five years in the instruments that measure ratings (Ibope Net Ratings, Media Metrics, Júpiter, etc.), as well as tools to follow campaign performance, making this a more professional media and consequently stimulating the advertising market.

Different from the rest of the market, at Fischer América, Internet planning is performed within the agency, by media professionals. This media is considered within the global strategic recommendations of the advertiser, and not as a separate matter. All follow-up on the campaign performance is also done by the account manager, putting the advertiser at ease concerning possible tactical changes that may be deemed necessary in the course of the campaign.

Charts

Television and radio are the media with the largest penetration in all population segments (see graph below), and are present in 87.9 percent and 86.8 percent of Brazilian households, respectively:

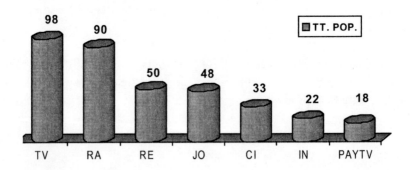

Radio

One week of programming, with 50 percent participation in ratings in the general public, on the principal stations and Brazilian state capitals:

	Stations	Ins	Cost 30" R$	Cost 30" US$	Reach %	Frequency X
São Paulo	10	300	286,449	99,496	52.6	7.0
R. Janeiro	8	220	157,546.95	54,723	51.0	6.0
Brasília	4	95	32,671.93	11,348	-	-
Porto Alegre	6	185	26,137.54	9,079	51.3	5.4

Cinema

Programming for one cinema week for 30" in an ideal number of major theaters for an efficient coverage:

	Recommended Number of Theaters	Cost 30" R$	Cost 30" US$
São Paulo	45	81,000	28,135
R. Janeiro	30	54,000	18,757
Brasília	25	45,000	15,630
Porto Alegre	14	25,200	8,753

Internet

Programming for 1 million printings, in the full banner format, on the home pages of the three major Brazilian portals:

	Printings	Total – Full Banner Home Page R$	Total – Full Banner Home Page US$
UOL	1,000,000	60,000	20,841
TERRA	1,000,000	65,000	22,577
IG	1,000,000	62,000	21,535

Unique visitors: an average of 11.3 million in each portal

Magazine

Cost, total number of readers, and circulation of the major general interest titles of weekly publications:

	Paid Circulation BR	Total Readers	Cost Simple Page	
			R$	US$
Veja	1.106.000	4.381.000	145.000,00	50.365
Época	440.000	1.908.000	79.700,00	27.683
Istoé	377.000	1.640.000	68.300,00	23.724

Newspapers

Major regional titles in the major Brazilian state capitals:

Markets / Newspapers		Paid Circulation (000)		Total Readers (000)		Cost 1 Pag. BW R$		US$	
		Sun	Wk days	Sun	Wk days	Sun	Wk days	Sun	Wk days
S.Paulo	Estado de SP	295	224	861	1.044	320.736,00	226.200,00	111.405	78.569
S.Paulo	Folha de SP	375	298	886	1.352	331.344,00	226.200,00	115.090	78.569
R.Janeiro	O Globo	370	239	1.244	1.212	257.088,00	151.632,00	89.298	52.668
Brasília	Correio Braziliense	89	49	592	429	63.960,00	42.744,00	22.216	14.847
Porto Alegre	Zero Hora	252	169	730	659	32.274,00	21.780,00	11.210	7.565

The average income determines the social class of the individual and of the household. For example:

The target normally considered in media planning is composed of men and women above the age of twenty-five in the ABC social classes, which characterizes the so-called "opinion formers."

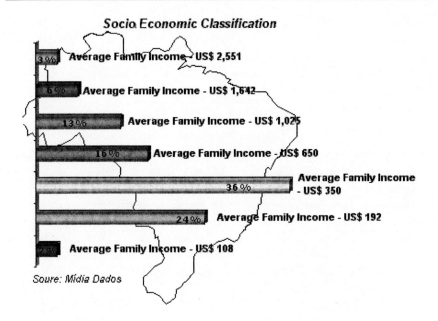

Soure: Mídia Dados

Conclusion

The economic crisis throughout the world and especially in Latin America has made people suffer. The tendency is for advertising to go back and use more humor with intelligence. Happy people make advertising work.

I believe there is a movement today towards bringing back efficient ideas for advertising. What we have learned from the last economic crisis is that efficiency must be present within the creative ideas. But it is not enough to have an incredible idea that does not sell. So, effectively, what is going to change is the joining of creativity with strategy, the focus on results. Today, things are going this direction, and in the near future, this will be a much valued and demanded requirement by the advertising market.

Eduardo Fischer is one of the most renowned Brazilian creatives. In his twenty-three-year career, he conquered more than 600 of the most important awards in advertising and built one of the main advertising agencies in Brazil, Fischer America, elected in 1997 by Advertising Acts as the fourth best in the world. In 1999, it was the most awarded agency at the Cannes Film Festival, and in 2002, Fischer was elected Agency of the Year by the Premio Columnistas (Columnists' Award). In 2004, Fischer received the 2003 Agency of the Year Award from the ABP (Brazilian Advertising Association) and the 2004 Premio Abril de Publicidade (Abril Advertising Award) in the "Reader's Opinion" category.

Mr. Fischer has been elected Advertising Person of the Year five times and represented Brazil as juror for the Clio Awards in Amsterdam and New York, and twice at SAWA in Cannes.

In 2004, he received the Professional Contribution Prize by APP (Advertising Professionals Association), and was elected agency director professional for his innovative acting at the advertising agency and contribution to the professional upgrade of the market. Presently, Mr. Fischer is president of Fischer America and Grupo Total de Comunicação —the holding company controlling the net of Fischer America agencies, present in ten Latin American countries and other companies in the communications sector. For his performance in the area, he was chosen as the Latin American Advertising Person in 1996 by the Latin American Advertising Agencies Association. He was the only Latin American entrepreneur to participate as spokesman at the forty-sixth World Federation Advertisers Congress in Seoul, Korea in 1999. In the same year, he was elected business leader by the subscribers of the Gazeta Mercantil *newspaper, the most traditional publication of economy and business in Brazil.*

China and Hong Kong

Michael Wood
Chief Executive Officer, Greater China
Leo Burnett Ltd.

China is not one single market, but is rather a number of provinces with different rules and regulations. For this reason, it is often difficult to establish national brands in many categories. The key to building brands in China is focus. Start small and build on success. The market is complex, so "don't bite off more than you can chew." Many marketers have failed in China because they have spread their resources too thin trying to accomplish too much too quickly. Marketers must continue to learn, learn, and learn more about the consumers in China. Understanding to whom you are selling is no different than in any other market, but it is made more complicated in China because of the geographic size and diversity of the country. Also, because the industry is developing, access to accurate and insightful information can be difficult. Innovation in research is key to understanding Chinese consumers.

Having a clear, focused idea (business and creative) of what your brand will stand for and then executing that idea throughout the entire brand experience is key to success. Execution is everything. Marketing solutions are delivered on a path from "thought to reality." Grand ideas (thought) are worthless if you don't have the means to execute communication programs throughout the brand experience (advertising, retail, packaging, events, public relations, etc.) down to the last deal (reality). Therefore, keeping ideas and consequent programs simple and ensuring that they are well executed to a high standard are key to the impression your brand will leave on people.

The advertising industry in China is only about twenty-five years old and has only experienced real development over the past fifteen years. Media is still largely state-owned with strong censorship regulations. China is also one of only a handful of communist countries in the world. It also has the largest population with one of the world's fastest growing economies. The combination of these factors present significant growth opportunities in a country that is relatively new to brands, where there is a significant influx of foreign brands and new technologies.

Advertising can tend to be focused on driving awareness because bigger (as judged by media spend) is deemed better by consumers in terms of quality. So many marketers are more focused on getting a brand name out than building the core values behind that brand.

China Is...

Because brands and advertising in China are still a relatively new concept compared with other more developed economies, there are a number of dynamics that have an impact on how advertising works. First, most categories are not as cluttered with brands as they are in more developed markets. Brands tend to be more mass market; as a consequence, brand owners try to build volume where it exists and there are nowhere near the level of niche brands. As a result, awareness is extremely important to get brand names to the top of mind. This is particularly important for foreign brands that may be new to the market. With all that being said, China is not developing with normal product category lifecycles that have allowed consumers to be educated slowly over time as to the benefits of products in a category.

People have gone from no landline telephone to the latest, most compact mobile phone that includes everything from MP3 players to cameras to SMS capability. The same exists in many other categories where consumers have experienced an unbelievably condensed category development lifecycle. As a result, it is critical for marketers to really understand the key insights about the people they are selling to and identify what are the core benefits that will meet their needs (these may be needs they can't articulate), and then create communication that brings those benefits to life in a real and meaningful way. Success means not taking for granted that the inherent benefits may be obvious.

This does not lead directly to boring educational advertising, but it reinforces the need not to overlook the obvious. For example, the incidence of washing hair is low in China relative to some other markets. To market a shampoo, it is important to understand the core motivation that may get someone to wash his or her hair, and then portray that in a human and believable manner.

Theoretically, advertising in China works exactly the same as it does in any market. It is all about understanding the people you are selling to and what will connect them with your brand—bringing that connection (benefit) to life through an advertising idea that will deeply resonate with those people in their lives. Inspire and excite them through communication that brings that idea to life and remain consistent to that idea through all facets of the brand experience. The dynamics of the market in China are different as outlined above, but the principles remain the same. The key to success is understanding the dynamics in a way that allows you to apply the principles.

The basics of advertising in China start with understanding Chinese people ("consumers" being those people you want to sell to) and identifying their core motivations for using products in your category. Why do they use your category? How do they use your category? On what do they make a brand choice? This should give insight into their lives as it relates to your category. You must understand how your brand is going to connect with those consumers on a functional level, but also on an emotional level. Many people make the mistake of believing that because marketing is developing in terms of brands, people are therefore more rational or functional in how they choose brands. In fact, research has shown the opposite. Because consumers do not hold a legacy with brands in the market, they are more willing to accept product claims at face value, and it is an emotional connection that stimulates trial.

After articulating the platform that will connect consumers with your brand, it is key to build from that platform a creative idea that will bring the connection to life in a way that will truly resonate with Chinese consumers. That idea must then be communicated through advertising in a way that is fresh, engaging, and believable, such that it inspires trial in the immediate while building the reputation for the long haul. At the same time, it is key that the idea is consistently extended to all facets of the brand experience. Holistic programs that extend ideas to everywhere a consumer touches a brand are keys to success. This means ensuring that the packaging reflects the idea and imagery; it means ensuring that the communication in the retail environment and merchandising is in keeping with that idea; it means ensuring that all promotions, public relations, sampling, and events build on the same theme.

Simply because China is still developing in terms of brands both domestic and foreign, it is not an excuse to lazily believe that Chinese consumers will not notice the difference. All categories in China will become significantly more crowded over the coming years, and those that have taken the expedient route to short-term sales without consideration for establishing the brand values and reputation over the long term will find themselves lost in the clutter of commodity. By this time, the relative cost of building those values into your brand will cost tenfold. It will never be cheaper to build a brand in China than it is now.

Over the years that we have operated in China, we have conducted a significant amount of research into the types of advertising that works best among a Chinese audience. The results have debunked most of the commonly held myths that marketers hold about advertising to the Chinese.

In short, we know what works:

- *Show, don't tell.* Brand rewards or benefits need to be highly visible through demonstration, dramatization, lifestyle, feelings, analogy, metaphor, and so on
- *Link brand to the action.* The brand needs to be the major player in the experience, and the link between the brand and execution is clear (the scenario revolves around and highlights the brand).
- *Be single-minded.* The execution needs a focus. A "laundry list" of product benefits results in sensory overload, resulting in no clear message being taken away.
- *Find emotional connections.* Feelings need to be anchored to the needs and aspirations of the target consumer.
- *Strive for striking imagery.* Striking, dramatic imagery is characteristic of many successful executions, enhancing their ability to break out of the clutter.
- *Have a unique personality.* An original, creative signature or mystique exists in many of the best commercials to bond the consumer to the brand and give it a unique personality.
- *Be innovative.* The best creative ideas for mature brands often use fresh new ways of revitalizing the message.
- *Make people laugh.* When humor is used, it is relevant with a clear product purpose and it is not self-deprecating.
- *Wisely consider celebrities.* When celebrities are used, they are well matched to the brands and have credibility as users, and their delivery is believably enthusiastic.

- *Be careful with exaggeration.* Exaggeration, like humor, must be clever and used to stress a point, not cheat.
- *Search for the big idea.* Drama, big idea, story. (It doesn't mean a beginning, middle, or an end is needed.)

China Isn't...

Reading a few textbooks and articles and thinking you understand the Chinese would obviously be a mistake. China has a history longer than most countries, has more dialogues and ethnic origins, and is growing and changing faster than any other country. Investment in "consumer understanding" is not always on the top of companies' priorities when there are so many other costs for a business startup.

Think twice if you think that because China is a developing advertising market, all communication has to be dulled down to the lowest common denominator. This work is both lost in the clutter and quickly insulting to consumers. A lack of advertising savvy does not equate to a lack of intelligence or comprehension of marketing messages. Advertising in China today is not like advertising in the United States or the United Kingdom in the 1950s.

Another mistake would be to believe that television is enough to build awareness, and hence a brand. Television is important in China, and is the most powerful awareness medium, but sales success only comes when you start to get the product in people's hands. That means an emphasis on reaching out to consumers through sampling, communicating with them when they first come into contact with your product at retail, and making sure they are given an incentive to trial.

Here are just a few advertising myths in China that have proven to be far from the case in reality:

- "Chinese are literal in their understanding of advertising. They don't understand anything too clever, subtle, or creative, therefore we have to rely on literal advertising."

- "Chinese aspire to a lifestyle filled with luxury, glamour, elegance, and romance, therefore that's what we should reflect in our advertising."
- "Chinese need something straightforward; they don't think deeply about the hidden messages."
- "Chinese love lots of information, so put all the information in, even if it's a small super lasting for one second."
- "Chinese want to see positive things; creative with a negative approach never works."
- "Fantasy doesn't work with the Chinese."
- "The Chinese love celebrity endorsements more than anything, therefore celebrities are a must; if you don't have a celebrity, you don't have a chance."
- "Chinese prefer to see Chinese nationals promoting a product."
- "Only ads that reflect people's 'daily life' or 'real life' are relevant to Chinese."
- "Ad drama must have a beginning, middle, and end."

The biggest challenge in China is access to research in order to understand such a geographically, culturally, and economically diverse country that is rapidly developing. Consumers are being exposed to new products and categories at an expediential rate. People whose household income is increasing significantly year after year are thereby having the opportunity to consume in an increasing number of categories. Assimilating this vast amount of information into insightful and inspiring advertising strategies is one of the biggest challenges.

Another major challenge is the attraction and retention of top local talent. Because the market is relatively young, the pool of top local talent is in demand, and as such, attracting them is key to driving an advertising organization forward.

Educate local clients on the value of a brand over the long term beyond sales for the immediate present. In a market where year-on-year growth has continued to meet or exceed expectations, it is difficult to get local clients to invest behind building the value of their brand for the long term. Work with them to understand that the categories in which they operate in are becoming more cluttered and often commoditized every year, and it is only those brands which establish a strong reason for being in consumers' minds that will succeed in the future.

Getting the Message Across

Mass media advertising (television, press, radio) account for almost 50 percent of total category spends. The media breaks down as follows:

Television

Mass media spend is dominated by television due to the delivery of national coverage (CCTV) and strong city coverage (Shanghai, Chongqing, Beijing) and provincial coverage at high viewership levels. This medium provides the strongest medium by which to build awareness in the most cost-effective manner.

Newspaper

Newspaper is a high-penetration medium in most urban cities, with over 2,000 titles in China. Most general morning/evening papers are the mainstream in their targeting and editorial. There has also been a boom in special interest publications (e.g., information technology, finance, fashion, entertainment, etc.). On the whole, newspapers are fairly inflexible operations in advertising, with most being government-owned and under strict censorship. There is currently a lack of any circulation audits.

Magazines

There are more than 9,000 magazine titles in China, with more than 1,000 new magazines appearing in the past five years.

Radio

There are more than 1,900 radio stations in China, and they are continuing to expand to niche position areas in key cities (e.g., financial, music, kids, and traffic channels). Overall, most stations carry a contemporary broadcasting format that appeals most to youth. This medium provides many flexible buying opportunities for program sponsorships/syndication. However, there is a lack of research and limited monitoring of radio ratings and ad spend.

Internet

China is one of the fastest growing markets by Internet popularity. With 79.5 million online users, China is the biggest Internet market in Asia, ranked the second in the world. Though PC penetration is low in China (21 percent), Internet penetration will continue to grow with dual usage (home/work).

The Target Audiences

Media targeting in China currently is done on fairly rudimentary levels, given the lack of quality data. Most target audiences are defined in terms of demographic measures such as sex, education, occupation, income, and household size. This is also combined with geographic data such as tier-one, -two, -three cities or rural.

For the development of creative advertising, an overlay of psychographic information such as shared attitudes, beliefs, needs, and opinions towards a category is needed, but this will largely depend on access to proprietary research conducted by an agency or client.

By and large, this overlay of consumer understanding is most commonly used by foreign marketers such as Proctor & Gamble, Coca-Cola, Wrigley, Cadillac, McDonald's, and others who are making significant investments in research to understand Chinese consumers. However, more sophisticated local marketers are also starting to invest in this area, such as Li Ning, Lenovo, Haier, and TCL.

What We Do

Perhaps more than any other agency, Leo Burnett globally has a heritage of creating big, iconic brands that have consistently stayed relevant to generations of consumers. We do not define brands by ad campaigns or taglines. We define brands in terms of ideas that inspire people and foster enduring belief. In China, we have taken our global brand building methodology and evolved it for a market that is in the infancy of brand building, but nonetheless clients are aspiring to build "icon brands with a Chinese voice."

The best, most successful, and enduring brands stand above their competitors because they have created armies of believers. Disney, McDonald's, Nintendo, Heinz, and Kellogg's are some of the world's most valuable brands because people have gone well beyond merely buying them. These are brands people believe in.

Believers produce greater volume, are less price sensitive, stay with a brand longer, and advocate it to others. The relationship between a believer and a brand—a well-defined brand bond—is the underlying force that keeps them together. The key to sustaining belief is keeping the expression of that bond alive and relevant in the constantly changing marketplace. Our proprietary planning model, the Brand Belief System™, combines unique quantitative tools, strategic planning, and creativity to help identify believers, articulates the brand bond (what connects people with the brand), and develops brilliant ideas to keep that connection alive.

To build belief in a brand, the idea must excite and inspire people—grab their attention, pique their interest, arouse their emotions, and resonate with what they hold to be true.

To succeed, the brand needs both integrity and charisma. Integrity— consistent brand experience—creates and reinforces belief and makes it resistant to future change. Brands with integrity have symbols, actions, tone, packaging, and product experiences that reinforce each other. Belief is generated most strongly when an event or experience is imbued with emotion: that's the role of charisma. Brands with charisma repeatedly arouse emotion within the community of believers in a specific way that enhances belief.

How do we build belief in brands and create an army of brand believers? We identify a powerful brand bond (based on a deep understanding of consumers' deep motivations in the category), create a big brand idea that deeply resonates with people's existing belief systems, deliver it with a voice and message both arresting and believable (brand charisma), and act in a manner consistent with that idea throughout all facets of the brand experience (brand integrity).

Our approach is to understand the brand and the consumer, and then to uncover the most powerful unvarnished truth that connects them. Out of this alchemy, we create the brand idea which, when delivered through a brand's charisma and integrity, inspires enduring belief.

With the importance of understanding Chinese consumers, gaining insight and understanding of their deeper motivations for category and brand usage, we have worked with a global planning tool that drives that understanding. This is key to uncovering the connection between brand and consumer.

One of the more difficult aspects of building an "army of believers" is gaining insight into the deeper motives behind their use of the category and the brands they believe in. While people can talk about the needs with which they associate various brands and products, they typically express these in functional terms: convenient to use, tastes great, lasts longer. However, people also experience products and brands on much deeper and more emotional levels than the typical attribute or benefit response would suggest. Behind every "tastes great" lies a realm of hard-to-articulate or hard-to-admit motivations that we often miss in our quest for functional "points of difference."

Understanding these deeper motives associated with a product category helps to explain why people use the brands they do. Why does convenience or taste or durability matter? What deeper human needs and desires are fulfilled when a brand delivers on these? If we can understand this, then we can evaluate brands not just on a myriad of attributes, but also on the real "essentials" of the category—a critical step toward building believers.

Building an Icon Brand with a Chinese Voice

Li Ning, a Believer of "Anything is Possible," Winning More Believers of Its Own

The name Li Ning holds a twofold meaning—the Chinese Olympic gymnastics sensation who touched the hearts of millions, and the sports brand that many increasingly consider to be the pride of Chinese brands. Today, it would not be surprising if the latter comes to mind first and receives more approving nods.

Its Beginning as a Follower, Backed by a Sports Legend

Li Ning, the sports brand, has its beginnings in the year 1990. During a time when the China sports goods market was a playground for big foreign brands like Nike and Adidas, Li Ning did not have big buzzwords like "the latest design" or "the most advanced technology." In those early days, Li Ning took the safe route by producing mid-priced sports goods that imitated the designs of the market leaders on the outside while offering mediocre quality on the inside—a strategy that worked well at that time. Li Ning himself was the spokesperson for the brand. The sponsorship deal for the China Olympic team during the early 1990s greatly helped to raise awareness of the brand in the second- and third-tier markets.

Moving Beyond Its Own Heritage, Hurdles to Overcome

In 1999, Li Ning incorporated the vision of becoming a global brand into its corporate agenda. It was during that same time that the increasing pressure from international players made Li Ning realize that stronger measures were required for the brand to take off. It began developing its own designs through the hiring of top French designers, and enriched its product portfolio to target different consumer segments.

Notwithstanding the fact that the portrayal of Li Ning as the "national hero" sports brand helped attract more consumers in the short run, this approach was a result of profit-driven reactive strategies that compromised what the brand stood for—thereby creating enormous confusion among consumers.

To rectify this, Li Ning focused on projecting a more approachable brand personality by moving away from the national hero image.

Becoming a Believer of Long-Term Brand Building

After revisiting its ambition to compete on the world stage, the company recognized the value of brand building in the long run—which called for trading off its original profit-centric strategy. In 2002, Li Ning joined hands with Leo Burnett Beijing to develop branding campaigns that helped to cultivate an enduring belief in the brand (i.e., a belief so strong that it forms an unbreakable bond between the consumer and the brand so that it becomes the constant preferred choice in their minds).

What the brand needed to do was identify a prominent consumer need and convince consumers that it was the only solution to that need. To begin with, a survey was conducted to understand unmet consumer needs in the market. The study revealed that the future holds a mixed picture for the Chinese consumers: on the macro level; they feel optimistic about the country and enjoy an upwardly mobile trend anticipated to last for the next ten to twenty years at the very least. This is especially so with the 2008 Olympics and the 2010 World Expo. On the other hand, they fear failure on a personal level and feel insecure about withstanding competition in the marketplace. Nevertheless, the positive fact is that this would gradually diminish as the overall societal conditions continue to improve over time. To conclude, the road ahead is generally fruitful to the Chinese people, as long as they put in honest efforts to earn the rewards.

The Campaign Developed by Leo Burnett Beijing

When matching the brand's ambitious global vision and relentless pursuit of dreams against the optimism of the Chinese people, an all-encompassing powerful proposition is born: "*Anything is possible.*" In the sports context, it makes a strong statement that true sports can happen anytime anywhere: it develops one's unlimited potential, it can either be serious or casual, it's a new way of living that brings pleasant surprises to life, it removes restrictions and allows freedom, and so on. What is more life inspiring is that it articulates the essence of the brand as one that empowers people to believe in themselves and never give up on their ultimate dreams.

First Phase:

With the platform being set, a holistic thematic television commercial and print ad campaign is rolled out in 2002, riding on the creative idea that "The world is one big stadium, as long as you want it to be. Li Ning, anything is possible." The stories unfold amid casual settings, which were being used as training grounds by ordinary sports players. The campaign was complemented by a provocative statement: "Who says not possible?"

Second Phase:

Building on the same concept, the brand continued in 2003, a related but even more exciting campaign based on the creative idea, "Say goodbye to yesterday's records. Li Ning, anything is possible." This campaign proved to be more vibrant and energetic, portraying determined young people bravely challenging old records, accompanied by punchy statements like, "Goodbye, XL/bench/last year's champion."

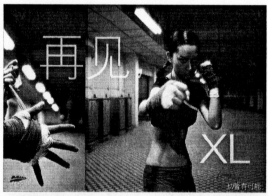

Third Phase:

Capitalizing on the ever-growing national pride around the country during the period when the announcement came in 2004 that China was hosting the 2008 Olympics, the campaign took the branding effort further with the idea, "Anything is possible when we Chinese work together." The idea was brought to life by powerful illustrations of Chinese athletes focusing on the games and creating miracles at the Olympic stadiums, with the headline, "The same heartbeat/The same bloodline. Made in China."

Other Material Developed Under the Campaign

Prior to the brand's initial public offering in Hong Kong, a series of print ads were produced to demonstrate Li Ning's success and uncompromising spirit rooted in China. The compelling images of Chinese athletes pushing their own limits combined with the headline "Li Ning, flying high in Chinese sports" created big buzz and confidence in the brand.

In 2004, Li Ning also demonstrated its understanding of the Chinese consumers by coming up with the television commercial series featuring Li Tie, a famous Chinese athlete, with the message that "Fits Chinese feet better," as well as the imagery point of sale materials, elaborating the point that, "We study Chinese, and we're made for Chinese."

Sticking to its Belief Pays Off on the Scoreboard

Just like dedicated training is more likely to yield better scores, the continuous brand building efforts Li Ning put in paid off in many ways:

- The post-2003 thematic campaign survey shows a clear outtake of the key message "Anything is possible," with an improved brand personality of sporty, confident, young, and Olympic. Consumers also echo a high brand affinity (87 percent), trustworthiness (88 percent), and uniqueness (84 percent). All in all, sales gained an impressive 30 percent.
- The brand's top-of-mind awareness and unaided/aided awareness ranked second in the China market, a close match against the international giant Nike.
- The brand's sales performance throughout 2003 is considerably higher compared to 2001 and 2002.
- The Litie soccer boots television commercial yields higher top-of-mind, aided and unaided awareness over Nike and Adidas.
- The brand was ranked China's "third coolest" local brand among university students.
- The campaign has raised many eyebrows around the globe throughout 2004, proving that the brand has taken the right track on its way to success.

Other Key Success Factors

Cooperation with multinational partners such as an international-level agency, research houses, and consultants, coupled with company operation of international standards, have helped the brand establish a strong international image. On the same note, strategic sponsorship of international teams was also one of the key factors that helped raise the brand's image on an international level. This is best illustrated by the sponsorship of the Spanish men's basketball team's uniform during the 2004 Olympics, where they went on to defeat the China team.

The Sky is the Limit

Taking into consideration that international names like Nike and Adidas have always been giving their best to increase their presence in China, Li Ning makes yet another strategic move in 2005 by partnering with the National Basketball Association (NBA) in its marketing within China. By now, Li Ning is truly competing with these international giants on a level field on the NBA court. Winning this battle would therefore be critical to the success of the brand. A series of television commercials featuring the NBA partnership are due to be launched on national television shortly.

With China hosting the 2008 Olympics, the perfect stage is awaiting this brave athlete to outperform foreign players for the gold medal in front of the whole world.

Calendar of Events

1990   Li Ning sports goods brand established
1992-96   Sponsored the China Olympic team; became the exclusive sponsor for China's gymnastics, diving, ping-pong, and shooting teams
1999   Incorporated "becoming an international brand" into the corporate vision
2000   Joined hands with nine European countries to establish overseas shops
            Became the Olympic sponsor of the French gymnastics association
2001   Signed contracts with top French and Italian designers to raise standards of its sports outfits
            Sponsored the Russian National Team at the International University Games at Beijing
            Established the first overseas branded stores in Spain, established the first sports accessories store in Xiamen
            Held numerous competitions in conjunction with other companies, such as the "Challenge Your Limits" competition with Philips
2002   Handed its advertising task to Leo Burnett, with the key objective being brand building

	Launched the first advertising campaign on the "Anything is possible" platform
	Sponsored the Spanish national team at the World Female Basketball Championship Tournament
2003	Launched the second advertising campaign on the "Anything is possible" platform upon the success of the first campaign
2004	Became listed on the Hong Kong stock market
	Launched the third advertising campaign on the "Anything is possible" platform
2005	Becomes marketing partner of the NBA in China

Getting Beyond the Superficial Connection

Innerview™ Motivation was designed to address these issues, by answering two fundamental questions. First, at a level deeper than functional attributes and benefits, what do people really want from the category? And second, how well does a particular brand deliver on these?

In building brand belief, it's not just important to know *whom* your current and potential believers are, but also *how* to build belief. Though difficult to elicit, deep motives illuminate valuable human connections that are often the cornerstone of why a current believer believes or that, once understood, can serve as a powerful lever to getting a potential believer to believe. In an atmosphere of increasingly limited, subtle, or easily replicated functional differences, the attributes and benefits we strive to carve out as our brand's turf are, in reality, rarely ownable in and of themselves. But frequently, the motivational terrain connected with them is and, once claimed, the high ground of these deeper human connections is tougher territory for a competitor to preempt, so the advantage often goes to the brand that stakes the first claim and gets it right. Not surprisingly, brands that build these deeper human connections have a real advantage in drawing potential believers into the franchise, as well as in making it more difficult for a competitor to lure current believers away.

By having a tool that can facilitate the study of motivations, the result is a clear understanding of what really matters to your most valuable targets, leading to an improved opportunity for more focused brand positionings and communication content.

Innerview™ Motivation was created to overcome these challenges. Based on a proprietary framework of human motivation, the important drivers of behavior have been captured in a rich lexicon of language, which is tapped to create a customized study for a brand. Leveraging both the framework and the lexicon, an Innerview™ study provides clarification of the deeper things consumers want from a category and quantification of how well a particular brand fulfills these.

People use products and choose brands to fulfill needs and accomplish goals in their lives.

At the most basic level, products are tools that enable us to mold, shape, and move smoothly along with our lives, while brands provide an array of options for how we want this process to occur. If you ask, people can talk about the needs with which they associate various brands and products, though usually in functional terms.

Knowing the attributes and benefits associated with product use and brand choice is essential to understanding a brand, and has long been an important element of usage and attitude and tracking studies. However, because people also experience products and brands on deeper and more emotional levels, their responses, when probed more deeply, are telling.

The "Motives Lexicon" is the engine that powers the customized Innerview™ Motivation studies we conduct. It's organized as a map around two simple summary dimensions, applicable to any product or brand:

Does using the product or brand (in whatever situations apply) primarily help me enhance my individual desires and well-being, or is it more about helping or contributing to the well-being of others—friends, family, or society as a whole? (self-focused versus other-focused)

When I use the product or brand, is my goal more about pursuing change, growth, or new experiences, or is it more about maintaining things the way they are and creating a level of security, stability, and pattern? (growth versus stability)

Based on the space created by these two initial dimensions, all kinds of human motives can be organized around the map at progressively more specific levels. At the most summary level, the lexicon is organized into twelve general areas of motivation. Beneath each of these twelve are numerous and more specific subgroups of motivation. Finally, beneath each of these are lists of motivational language people use to describe the particular dimensions. The illustration below shows how the Lexicon is organized. Responsibility, for example, one of twelve major "summary level" motive categories, contains many subtler subcategories (such as work ethic), and within each of these are many specific motives, such as "being the kind of person who can get things done." In like fashion, each of the twelve major categories is backed by multiple, subtler levels of motives.

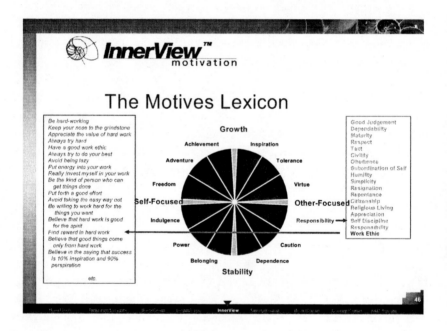

Measuring Marketing Success in China

Success in China is largely measured in four core areas:

- *Sales performance:* Based on the achievement of annual sales targets, advertising is judged to be effective in driving the business. Obviously, as in other markets, there are many other components that drive sales beyond advertising, and therefore this should not be the sole measure of success.

- *Brand image and attribute goals:* Many larger clients now run annual or biannual image and tracking studies on their identified target to determine the strength of their brand relative to competition against a number of key measures they would like their brand to stand for in the minds of consumers. Once these measures have been benchmarked, it is then possible to set annual goals where a client's brand wants to achieve a level of variance versus competition.

- *Brand awareness:* Many clients are running awareness studies on their identified targets pre- and post-campaigns to measure top of mind awareness, unaided and aided brand recall. Again, once benchmarks have been established, it is then possible to track these measures on an ongoing basis.

- *Response rates:* This measure of success can be applied against any program that has a response mechanism. This may be attendance at an event, response to a sales promotion or competition, or response to an offer in a direct mail program. Again, given that there are no industry norms established for most of these disciplines, most clients who do use these measures for success will normally have to benchmark against themselves.

The Advertising Campaign

Leo Burnett (the man) described the goal of advertising as "creating sales in the immediate present while building a brand's reputation over the long haul." He said this back in the 1950s, and the goal is still the same today, only the method of communication may have evolved. The goal of any advertising campaign is to be based on a single-minded idea that connects with consumers and is communicated in a way that is fresh, engaging, and believable, while at the same time remaining consistent with that idea throughout all facets of the brand experience (i.e., everywhere people come in contact with the brand).

If I had an unlimited budget for a campaign, I would be able to deliver a brand message holistically through a variety of mediums that would touch people at all points during their purchase decision. For an automobile, that may be television to drive awareness of the marque, press to communicate specific features of a certain model, strategic outdoor to keep the model top of mind when consumers are out driving, and direct mail to present an offer for a test drive to bring the brand experience to life in the showroom. Infinite budget is about being able to impact every step in the purchase decision.

If money were limited, on the other hand, I would focus on television, which is still the most cost-effective medium in China. The media can be targeted to specific target audiences in specific geographical areas to increase impact. As a medium, television is still the most persuasive and impactful communication tool. The tighter the budget, the greater the need for a simple and impactful idea that can be produced in a visual manner. Nothing moves hearts like television, and in China nothing speaks a louder volume as to the quality perception of a brand than television. In China, it always has been, and remains today, a powerful way to connect with consumers.

The Role of Technology

China is one of the fastest growing markets for Internet popularity. With 79.5 million online users, up 34.5 percent from 59.1 million users one year earlier, China is the biggest Internet market in Asia, ranked second in the world. Though PC penetration is low in China (21 percent), Internet penetration will continue to grow with dual usage (home/work). The Chinese government is using the Internet to disseminate information to the general population, and this is assisting in pushing usage.

Penetration of the Internet significantly increases when looking at the key tier-one cities. Usage is driven by e-mail, news, research, and chat rooms as opposed to e-commerce, but the medium provides a significant marketing opportunity.

Brands are using the Internet beyond simple banners. Brands are providing branded content within existing sites, using the medium for promotions via mini-sites, using it to deliver direct consumer one-on-one marketing communication.

Best Advice Received

To best understand China, you must understand where it has come from in order to understand where it is going. Many people look at China today and see the opening up of the economy as a sign that China is rapidly moving toward capitalism as we know it in the West. China is moving toward a more market-driven economy, but within the framework of a collective and nationalistic ideology. In order for many to live a better life, a few will experience greater prosperity initially as the economic development of China spreads throughout the country.

By understanding where China is going, you are able to better understand the Chinese people who are driving the development. Understanding Chinese people is the key to developing better advertising.

My Advice to Others

I have three pieces of advice on the China market, advertising in China, and simplicity in communication:

- For most of our clients, it's not about 1 billion-plus consumers, it's about the 160 million-plus urban households and the people who make up those households. It is the collective income of those households that is fueling the market for consumer and durable goods. Plans and goals should be prepared and built on gaining a share of those household purchases.
- Just because a market is developing, you do not have to develop advertising to the lowest common denominator. Everybody has needs, opinions, attitudes, beliefs, and aspirations for a better life. By creating communication that entertains, informs, and inspires, we can make our clients' brands part of the fabric of people's lives.
- Utilize the KISS principle (Keep it simple, stupid). Do not overcomplicate your message so that it becomes part of the incomprehensible clutter that is Chinese advertising today. Always make sure your advertising is single-minded in its focus to connect people with a brand in a manner that most resonates with their lives.

Advertising in China: A Recent Timeline

Public Wants More (1990s)

Urban Chinese had money and were willing to spend it. Other than through advertisements, nobody was telling them how to do it.

Research showed that Chinese ads had unfavorable responses in such areas as amusing, artistic, intelligent, and memorable.

Ads Are No Big Deal Anymore (1990s)

In 1992, there were 16,652 advertising companies in China (compared to 6,052 in 1985).

On January 25, 1993, the *Shanghai Wen Haui Bao* used the whole front page for an ad for an air conditioner company (Shi Ling), and people accepted it easily. Suddenly, advertising was no big deal.

Emphasis on Education (1990s)

The thinking was that consumers couldn't get enough information, so ads tried to take advantage of this "insight."

Expansion and Control (1990s)

By 1995, CCTV launched five new channels and Shanghai Television expanded with one new station (OTV).

Television advertising became the number-one industry earner in China.

The Shandong liquor company Qing Shi paid 320 million RMB to CCTV for primetime space versus 66 million for the same amount in the previous year.[2]

---

[2] Premium time is between the weather report and the nightly news.

In 1996 there were:
2,235 newspapers (versus 188 in 1980)
8,000 magazines (versus 2,000 in 1980)
980 television stations and 1,200 cable stations (versus 202 television stations in 1980)

The government introduced a new advertising law.

Brand Building Blitz (1990s)

By 1997, there were 800 ads a week on Chinese television.

Consumers faced choices between brands that were not drastically different in function and quality.

People began to have a broader information channel and broader choices to satisfy their own consumption habits.

Advertising Today (2000+)

Today, advertising is considered by some to be even more interesting than the television programs.

More established brands are moving towards humor, emotion, and thought-provoking ideas over just functional benefits.

Coming Changes

With the Olympics set to take place in Beijing in 2008 and the government investing $45 billion in infrastructure towards the games, China will see a significant increase in marketing investment during that period by both official sponsors and non-sponsors, by local and foreign brands, and by all industries. These Olympics will be a showcase event like no other, for the first time putting China on the world sporting stage, and this will provide a huge platform for brand marketing.

With this increase in marketing and advertising investment, we would expect that there will be an increased investment in research with an improvement in the quality of both consumer and media research data. Although currently local clients are not heavy research investors, this will start to change as the investment in marketing and advertising, and the demand for more tangible results, increases. To this end, we are going to see more scrutiny of advertising performance with clients looking for increased accountability for investments. This will lead to better sales and market share data, which are both currently weak.

As the media industry becomes more competitive and therefore fragmented, we expect to see a significant increase in the flexibility of stations and publications toward creative media opportunities. As marketers become more sophisticated, so will the offerings of the media. In addition to offering the viewership, data will be needed to measure the elative performance of different mediums.

Over the next five years, we will see a significant expansion by many marketers beyond the tier-one cities on the Eastern seaboard into tier-two and -three cities and the rural community with different product offerings and packaging, which will be supported by different marketing and communication programs (e.g., small size or single usage/servings that increase trial but minimize cost outlay per purchase).

The rapid development of the Internet in China will continue to have a profound impact on Chinese people, both as members of society and as consumers. Word of mouth has always played an important role in Chinese society, where information is important to gaining credibility and trust. The technology of the Internet is providing the modern-day word of mouth through the massive dissemination of information. This is being driven from many different sources: government to people, marketers to people, people to people. People in China have access to information domestically and internationally like at no other point in history. Well-informed people make well-informed consumers. This will have a significant impact on how people accept brands in the future.

We will see significantly more products developed specifically for Chinese consumers across a wide range of categories as China becomes one of the dominating markets globally in that category. Gone are the days of passing the old models or minimal feature designs to China. The power and opportunity of the market necessitates that manufacturers are developing products specifically for Chinese consumers, and much has been written about the BRIC markets (Brazil, Russia, India, and China) and the impact they are having on product development and design. This means an investment in local research and development in China. This will also have a flow of effect on local brands in China that are not known for their investment in research and development. This is a significant competitive advantage for foreign brands, given their history of investment in research and development. Local brands are going to have to increase investment in this area if they are to compete with foreign brands over the next decade. What this means for advertising is significantly more local marketing where China is leading the world in products and campaigns that are developed for China rather than using ideas adapted from elsewhere.

This in turn will develop talent in all facets of the industry from consumer planning, to business management, to creative development, to production talent such as local commercial directors and photographers. This talent will come in high demand, and staff development and retention will become of paramount importance to advertising agencies.

There will be an establishment of some powerhouse Chinese brands in some key segments. These companies exist today and are in the process of brand building. Today, they have sales volume built on the back of superior local distribution versus competition. They have created brand name recognition and awareness, but are yet to establish real connection with consumers, which will happen over the next five to ten years. Currently, that group includes brands such as Haier, TCL, Lenovo, Li Ning, Wahaha, and Tsingtao.

Lastly, there will be an increase in one-to-one relationship marketing, which is currently still in its infancy as a discipline. This is currently driven by the lack of accurate databases and commercially available lists, but as clients start to build their own databases this will become a more commercially viable medium. This will also be helped by the ever-increasing penetration of the Internet.

Michael Wood is the chief executive officer of Greater China for Leo Burnett Ltd.

Germany

Marcus H. Starke
Chairman and Chief Executive Officer
PUBLICIS Frankfurt

The Basics of Advertising in Germany

In Germany, as in other major European markets, the most common advertising methods are classical advertising, direct marketing, public relations, sales promotion, sponsorships, new media, and event marketing.

The classical media are still very strong, but direct response, customer relationship management, and public relations are gaining in importance. In 2003, the market shares of classical media were as follows: radio (5 percent), posters (3 percent), daily papers (24 percent), magazines (22 percent), television (44 percent), and professional journals (2 percent). After a few years of almost complete silence after the dot-com bubble exploded, the Internet has come back and today is also part of the media mix in most advertisers' media plans.

Target markets are segmented by demographics, spending capacity, consumer acceptance, and lifestyle. The German consumer is very rational; therefore, fact-based creativity usually works well in advertising.

Foreign advertisers sometimes make the mistake of applying the same rules and principles as in their home markets, and thus fail to achieve relevance for the local market. This often is the case for international campaigns that have to meet local tastes and expectations that are sometimes substantially different from market to market.

Holistic Communication

To grow our clients' business, we work on the principle of "the holistic difference." This is our mission statement and working practice (i.e. the way we develop and implement successful communication strategies). It is the PUBLICIS approach for relevant, differentiating, and consistent brand communication that results from a holistic understanding of the brand and its relationship to the target groups, identifying and using the relevant contact points in order to ensure an effective development of the brand. It helps us to find out where, when, and how to connect to the consumer, and thus how to create an effective communication strategy. Our method is characterized by a workshop approach, collaboration between marketing communication experts, and collaboration with the client team. There are three stages to the development of communication campaigns: the brand workshop (in which we relate communications objectives to business objectives, define key audiences, understand the audiences' current perceptions of the brand, and generate potential brand ideas and concepts), the connection workshop (in which we understand and evaluate what channel connections the audience has with the product sector and brand), and the data workshop (in which we measure the effectiveness of the holistic plan).

When the budget is generous, my favorite communication strategy is a holistic communications campaign that has a relevant message for each contact point based on one strategy. When the budget is tight, I like to use direct response advertising and/or direct marketing.

We measure success by the attitude and the action taken by our target audience. Our goal for any communication campaign is to reach the target in the most efficient and effective way, provoking the desired action and/or attitude. We measure the return on advertising investment based on change of attitude and behavior, in addition to traditional measurements.

One of the biggest challenges we face is the increasing communication overkill and media explosion. Because of this, we need to be single-minded and straightforward, and keep our messages simple. The best advertising advice I ever received was to "Reduce to the max."

Changes and Trends in Communication

In the last five to ten years, changes in communication include the rise of comparative advertising, interactive, laws against tobacco advertising and increasingly in categories like alcoholic beverages, increased brand advertising, and advertising focused on different lifestyles. In the future, I believe we'll see more marketing aimed at seniors and various other cultural groups.

Also, clients increasingly expect their agencies to be business partners who are not just focused on delivering successful communication, but who truly understand the client's business and can contribute, help, and advise beyond just communications.

Major News Outlets

Newspapers:
- *Frankfurter Allgemeine Zeitung (FAZ)*
- *Bild Zeitung*
- *Süddeutsche Zeitung*

Magazines:
- *Der Spiegel*
- *Stern*
- *Focus*

News Wires:
- DPA
- DDP
- Reuters

Television Networks:
- ARD
- ZDF
- RTL Group
- Sat1ProSieben Media AG

Internet:
- www.spiegel.de
- www.netzzeitung.de
- www.faz.net

Languages Spoken:
- German
- English

Useful Advertising-Related Resources

Books:
Philip Kotler (*Grundlagen des Marketing*)
Heribert Meffert (*Marketing*)
Karl Schneider (*Werbung*)
Hans Weis (*Marketing*)
Roger Fisher (*Das Harvard-Konzept*)

Web sites:
www.wuv.de
www.gwa.de
www.horizont.net
www.zaw.de

Marcus H. Starke is chairman and chief executive officer of PUBLICIS Frankfurt, where he focuses on building a truly holistic communications agency that delivers communication strategies covering every aspect and discipline of modern communications. The vision for PUBLICIS Frankfurt is to become the best and most creative network agency in Germany.

Mr. Starke began his marketing career as an international product manager at Pirelli in Milan, followed by marketing positions with Star (Danone) in Milan and Cinzano (Diageo) in Geneva, Sao Paulo, and Turin. He returned to Germany to take a position as a management consultant with Gruber, Titze & Partners (Gemini Consulting) and then became a founder and managing partner of EMC Starke & Gerlach (European marketing consultants) and Idea Azione Promotions (diversified marketing services). After both companies were sold to Bates and assimilated into the Bates/141 Worldwide network (Cordiant Communications Group), Mr. Starke served as chief executive officer for Europe for 141 Worldwide, with responsibility for thirty-seven agencies providing integrated marketing communication services in thirty-one countries.

Mr. Starke's educational background includes a trainee program at Pirelli Deutschland, a business administration program at Berufsakademie Mannheim, and several post-university training programs, including at the Management Center Europe (Brussels) and INSEAD (Fontainebleu). He is fluent in German, English, Italian, Portuguese, and French.

Dedication: *To all the employees at PUBLICIS Frankfurt.*

Korea

Young Hee Lee
Chief Executive Officer
Diamond Ad

Highlights

Most Common Advertising Methods

- Celebrity-dependent creative (usually using celebrities from the entertainment industry)
- Repetitive messages (carpet bombing and reiteration)
- Movie/drama parody

How Advertising is Different in Korea

- In-house agencies comprise 80 percent of the industry
- Media buying system controlled by KOBACO (a government organization)
- Preliminary advertisement review system: Before an advertisement can be broadcasted to the public, the Korea Advertising Review Board's Advertisement Deliberation Committee ("the Committee") reviews the suitability of the relevant advertisement in consideration of relevant laws and regulations. The Committee deliberates on the broadcastability of the advertisement. It may make a conditional decision requiring partial touch or revision. After the Committee's approval, the advertisement is broadcasted through KOBACO.
- No partnership structure between agencies and clients; agencies are viewed as clients' subordinates.
- Clear distinction between corporate advertising and product advertising. (Clients—usually corporations—in the Korean market possess many subsidiary companies that span many different industries.)
- ATL-centered advertising; BTL is viewed as a byproduct of ATL (ATL: above the line, BTL: below the line).
- Clients are still in the early stages of implementing long-term strategies for increasing brand value; the majority of advertisements are geared toward achieving short-term business success, and long-term, goal-oriented, consistent advertising campaigns are still a rarity.

Three Keys to Successful Advertising in Korea

- Outstanding creative
- Appropriate advertising budget
- Consistent concept

Most Common Mistakes Made by Foreigners

- Lack of understanding of the precedence of personal relationships (based on family, regional, and educational background) over competence
- Lack of understanding of the precedence of flexibility (based on personal relationships) over contractual agreements
- Lack of understanding of the occurrence of inconsistent production, revision, and reproduction
- Abandoning advertising intentions due to excessive credit checks
- Management of advertising agencies by foreigners, not locals (chief executive officer and top management)

How News is Dispersed in Korea

Television is used for maximum speed and circulation, and newspapers for detailed information and interpretation. However, the importance of Internet news cannot be ignored in those sectors with high digital media access rates.

International Involvement

With the inflow of investment from worldwide communication groups, seven out of the top ten agencies in Korea have become international communication group companies. This trend is expected to continue in the future.

Overview of the Korean Advertising Industry

In the Korean advertising industry, in-house agencies, established by conglomerates, are positioned on top. Competitive pitches are frequent, but long-term agency contracts are rare. Integrated marketing services include creative and strategy development, production, media planning and buying, and below-the-line planning and execution. Unlike in foreign advertising markets, media specialty agencies are not very active in Korea. Current media agencies started off as the media departments of advertising agencies. The primary reason for this phenomenon is the existence of KOBACO (a government agency), which regulates the domestic media market.

Advertising in Korea is very client-oriented. We begin by establishing the communication and creative strategy, and then develop a concept for preliminary confirmation by the client. Further revisions are followed by presentation to the final decision-maker. The ad is then produced, and a preview is provided to the client with a final report for approval. The ad is then approved by the Advertisement Review Committee. The media buy is determined with the client's agreement, and then the ad goes on air.

Successful Advertising Methods

Two kinds of creative messages seem most successful with Korean audiences: (1) fun creative that delivers messages conveying family affection and love for nature, and (2) delivering messages through famous celebrity endorsement.

In terms of advertising methods, celebrity advertising is recognized as one of the most effective approaches. This method is used to naturally expose product benefits together with the celebrity appeal. There are many cases in which one celebrity is affiliated with more than one product. Consumer recognition of a brand or product image is closely related to the model's image. It is a common practice to have one or two representative celebrity models, but the multi-spot method (featuring a number of celebrities) is utilized for those clients with a sufficient advertising budget.

Carpet bombing and reiteration are also effective. Because most television ads run as fifteen-second spots, it is important to concentrate on delivering the core message. In order to achieve brand or product recognition in two to three months' time, identical messages are delivered repeatedly to consumers, with print, Internet, and other media used to supplement the process.

Movie/drama parodies are another common method. A parody of an entertainment or cultural phenomenon creates franchise power, which in turn has an impact on the product's credibility and appeal.

Target Markets and Advertising Costs

A target group is selected through cross-examination of consumer analysis (by age, sex, occupation, income, etc.) and psychological factors.

Companies in wireless communication services, electronics, automobiles, and cosmetics industries are the primary advertisers that target consumers between the ages of twenty-five and forty-nine. This target group possesses purchasing power, information dissemination power, and a strong craving for new information.

The cost of television advertising depends on the time, day, and program. Average costs are as follows: (1) prime-time spot ("SA" level): $8,350-$10,000, (2) "A" Level: $3,350-$6,700, (3) "B" Level: $1,670-$2,500, (4) fringe time ("C" Level): $850.

Newspaper costs vary based on classification (daily, economy daily, regional, etc.). The following rates are typical for a national daily's color print ad: (1) front page: $5,100 (five columns, approximately fifteen inches), (2) back page: $8,750 (full page), (3) other pages: $2,750 (five columns, approximately fifteen inches).

Magazine costs vary by media. The average rate for an inside ROP is approximately $2,500, but the price can change depending on a special position, the quality of the paper, and special printing processes. Premium prices are applied to back cover/inside front cover/inside back cover.

Diamond Ad's Services

We provide our clients with a wide range of services, including marketing communication strategy planning and execution; creative planning and production; media planning, buying, and efficiency analysis; promotion, event planning, sports marketing, and interactive marketing planning and execution; and D-CRM (Diamond Customer Relationship Management), an intranet service that provides advertising theory information, marketing case studies, completed advertisements, and advertising industry information.

One strategic tool we have designed to enable a scientific approach to media planning and measurement, and to secure the competitive edge of Diamond Ad's media department, is our media strategy system T-SMART (Total System Media Analysis and Research Tool). T-SMART was launched in February of 2003 after one year of development. Currently, many Korean agencies are competing to secure superior media systems, and major agencies are developing their own media systems or upgrading their existing systems. Media planning has become a competitive element, because media buying power determines the media power of an agency.

T-SMART is the first system in the industry to overcome the primary weakness displayed by other media systems, which is the inconsistency of different research companies' data. T-SMART has enhanced operational efficiency by enabling easy access through its user-friendly interface and providing superior execution speed and accurate information to Diamond's media team. However, in the future, the competitive edge of media is expected to shift from media systems to media specialists. In response to such expectations, T-SMART will be transformed from a specialist tool into a partner that provides media planning solutions for media specialists.

A second tool we have developed is the brand management model "Brand Odyssey." This is a systematic brand management model for developing ideas and creative, and executing media by analyzing the current brand or product status from the consumer's point of view. It reflects Diamond Ad's new corporate identity, "Think the Unthinkable." WPP, which possesses the know-how and experience to create and manage world-renowned brands, and Diamond Ad are collaborating to develop the model. Brand

Odyssey is composed of six parts: topographical survey, course examination, course selection, navigation, execution, and evaluation.

Finally, we have extensive consumer profile research. Started in 1992, our consumer survey has involved 6,000 consumers thirteen to fifty-nine years of age in twenty-one major cities. The information enables a comprehensive understanding of consumers and the development of marketing communication strategies through product utilization status data for 253 products, major media contact activities, and lifestyle analysis.

Facing Challenges and Measuring Success

One of the greatest challenges we face is clients' excessive participation in advertising strategy and creative (the initial expression of the strategy is greatly distorted by the time it reaches the execution stage). An extreme client/agency relationship can destroy the pride of advertising professionals. Declining agency revenue is another challenge.

At Diamond Ad, we measure our success in terms of maintaining long-term contracts, requests to participate in our clients' mid- to long-term marketing strategy development, and the achievement of client and brand image enhancement through the accumulation of success cases. We're also pleased when clients request that we participate in their overseas expansion as a master agency, or when clients request our consulting services in areas other than advertising.

Advertising Goals and Favorite Tools

The goal of an advertising campaign is selling everything. In that sense, advertising is both the science of selling products and the art that can move the deepest emotions of consumers. Art and science must be integrated through salesmanship. The heart of a poet plus the brain of a scientist plus the eye of an artist is a must. But most importantly, one must focus on extracting the targeted consumer response with the mindset of a businessman.

When there is a large budget, I like to concentrate on television media, considering its reach and credibility impact. Also, the four traditional major medias, a combination of new media tools, and a mixture of various below-the-line tools that can strengthen the consumer's brand experience.

When the budget is very tight, the approach depends on the brand's characteristics, the situation the client is facing, and the marketing target group. I like to develop epochal creative ideas that can overcome the budgetary constraints.

In measuring return on investment, we use GRP, CPM, and other media measurement figures. We analyze recognition and recollection rates, and consumer recognition and attitude variance rates. We also analyze the agency's contribution to achieving the client's marketing target by identifying changes in the client's sales volume, as well as analyzing the change in brand value.

The Internet and Technology

Approximately 30 million people (64.5 percent of the Korean population) are Internet users. Korea has one of the best Internet infrastructures in the world (the highest broadband access rate in the world), and the Internet media's credibility is rated second out of all media (television is rated first). Therefore, many companies are starting to use basic Internet homepages as a pillar of their marketing strategy. As of December of 2003, Korea's annual Internet advertising market had increased by 3 percent since December of 2002 to $200 million, and it is expected that the growth will continue.

Diamond is executing a variety of marketing activities, from securing marketing sources, to conducting online and offline customer relationship management activities, to increasing sales volume. Diamond was the first Korean advertising agency to create an Internet advertising team (1997). Diamond's Internet advertising team uses the Internet in various areas, such as securing a database that matches the client's marketing target and direction, branding the client or product, and executing cross-media sales and marketing programs.

Changes and Trends in Advertising

For most of the past thirty years, the Korean advertising industry maintained high growth rates. However, the Asian financial crisis in 1997 not only slowed down the growth rate, but also changed the paradigm of the advertising industry. Under the in-house structure, the Korean agencies were complacent and concentrated mainly on size expansion. But the merger and acquisition activity and reorganization fever of the financial crisis changed the face of the advertising environment and reformed the agencies into professional and competitive businesses.

There is greater allowance for comparative advertising and diverse creative attempts. During recessions and periods of economic hardship, advertisements that sport patriotic appeal, emphasize frugality, console the viewers, and concentrate on family affection seem to be the major trend. Also, analog and digital technologies now exert comparable impact on the creative. There has been significant change in the marketing environment (Internet, multimedia, multichannels, etc.).

Globalization has led to advertising agency mergers and acquisitions through the investment of foreign capital and global companies' aggressive penetration into the Korean market. In addition to consolidation through mergers and acquisitions, there has been an emergence of specialized agencies that concentrate on niche markets, and an acceleration of the specialization process of communication agencies. Although media management agencies have started to take form in the market, they are unable to exert significant influence because KOBACO regulates the media.

Looking forward, I see total competition in domestic and overseas markets. This will mean an increase in the importance of globalization, integrated services, and brand agency services. As more companies expand their operations overseas, it is important that agencies possess global operation capabilities. With unclear domestic economic prospects, the need for domestic companies to penetrate the global market is on the rise, and with the invasion of global communication holding companies, it is possible for domestic agencies to adopt the holding company system. Increased competition will mean that the rich get richer and the poor get poorer.

There will also be an increased emphasis on the role of brand guarding, which constructs and maintains a client's brand.

The media and consumer relationship will reverse. With the advent of multimedia and multi-channel options that enable the consumer to freely select the media of his or her choice, the market has shifted away from a mass system to a consumer-oriented system that can quickly respond to consumer demand.

In terms of agency operations, the emphasis in the future will be on return on investment. There will be a shift away from the commission rate system to a fee-based system that compensates the agency in accordance with the agency's contribution.

The digital nomads of the twenty-first century who live freely with digital devices will become a major target of advertising. There will also be greater emphasis on messages that invite the general public's participation and contribute to the public interest. Advertising will no longer be one-way communication.

Best Advice

The advertising advice I find myself giving others most often is "Think the opposite, think of insight, think of message, think of distinction." You have to think, act, and evaluate from the opposite point of view. Strive to find the consumer insight. The starting point of problem solving is finding the intuition that can move the logic. Deliver the creative that delivers live messages to the heart of the consumer and the market. Build brand power by pursuing the one percent differentiation that provides a unique brand attraction.

Before being promoted to the post of chief executive officer of Diamond Ad (the third largest advertising and marketing communications agency in Korea), Young Hee Lee served as the creative director of Diamond Ad. He has twenty-eight years of advertising experience, and he is the first chief executive officer with creative background in the Korean advertising industry.

Mr. Lee was named "2003 Advertiser of the Year" by Hankook Daily Newspaper. *He has received many awards from international advertising festivals (e.g. Cresta, London, New York) and served as domestic/international advertising festival judge (e.g. Good Advertisement Awards by Consumers, New York Int'l Festival, Clio Festival).*

Russia

Alexander Mozhaev
President
Znamenka Creative Agency

Highlights

Most Common Advertising Methods

- Television
- Print
- OOH (out of home)
- Various so-called below-the-line media (promos, events, POPM, etc.) and public relations are also gaining influence.

How Advertising is Different in Russia

- The advertising landscape is overly cluttered (especially in television and OOH).
- Storytelling (didactic messages) dominates over symbolism.

The Successful Advertising Strategy in Russia

- Very thorough consumer understanding
- Courageous, nontraditional approach to the message and vehicle
- Fair budgeting and consistency in communication

Most Common Mistakes Made by Foreigners

- "Foreign-ade" advertising for "locally-made" products
- Too much testing, which destroys the sharpness of the idea
- Trying to put several messages into one communication (Russians are quick, but the format is also short and there is too much information around)

How News is Dispersed

- General public: television news
- Specific target: various vehicles (including press, Internet, public relations, word of mouth)

Language(s) Spoken

- Russian
- English (business language): Generally, Russians are very keen on foreign languages; foreigners are often surprised to find out that their counterpart speaks Danish or Italian as well as English.

Major News Outlets

Newspapers:
- General: *Komsomolskaya Pravda, Izvestiya*
- Business: *Vedomosti, Kommersant*

Magazines:
- No one reads magazines for news

News Wires:
- Interfax
- RIA-Novosti
- Prime-TASS
- ITAR-TASS (mainly photo)

Television Networks:
- General: 1st channel, RTR, NTV
- Business: RBC
- Local: local channels

Internet:
- Lenta.ru
- Gazeta.ru

Successful Advertising

The types of creative approaches that seem to work best with a Russian audience are storytelling rather than just images, characters, and myths rather than just actors, humor (especially with national insight), and testimonials with an unusual twist. It is best to avoid goody-goody messages (people are tired of happy faces, especially "family in the kitchen" types of images).

If there is any guarantee for successful advertising, it is first and foremost digging for consumer insight. Discovering the strings of consumer mind and soul, and putting it in the center of creative idea, is the only means to make your advertising meaningful for consumers and therefore working for the brand and not only for the creator's ego, whether in the agency or with the advertiser.

We measure the success of our campaigns based on (1) the impact our ideas have on our clients' business, (2) whether our work is liked, both by the consumers and by the client and its referent group, and (3) advertising community appreciation (festivals, comments, ratings, etc.).

Challenges

The greatest challenges advertising agencies currently face are:

1. *Time pressure:* Every campaign (pitch) is done with very short deadlines, so working long hours and weekends becomes normal.
2. *Lack of qualified resources:* The industry is developing fast, and high schools are not currently able to supply enough high-quality newcomers.
3. Erosion of agency revenues: Two trends squeeze the agency— overall inflation, including for the staff, on one side, and a larger number of smaller accounts in the fee-based remuneration system on the other.

Changes

Looking back over the last ten years, there are two clear periods in advertising: before the 1998 crises and after. Both periods were characterized by dramatic (double-digit) growth at the end (1996–1997 and 2002–2003); however, during the second period, the growth was on a higher-quality level and was healthier, which reflects the fact that advertising is rapidly maturing. The biggest problem is the dominance of quantity and speed over quality and ideas—a focus that was dictated by rapidly growing demand.

Other current trends in advertising in Russia are:

- Specialization of services (more companies are set up in marketing services: merchandizing, event, product placement, sport marketing, etc.)
- Concentration of communication business in big holding companies (major international players strengthen their position in Russia: Omnicom, IPG, WPP, Publicis)

In the future, we must get ready for a slowdown in the industry and be prepared for the coming of the demand economy to Russia. At the moment, a good supply chain is enough for the majority of companies to prosper in the market. However, with market facilities improving (financial services, logistics, and transportation) and increasing of competition, any sustainable growth would be closely linked to the ability of a company to create long-term demand for their product. Consumers will avoid communicated messages, because there is too much information, and people have shorter attention spans and the capability to switch off. We must find clever ways to be relevant and create interaction in continually shorter moments of contact.

Alexander Mozhaev graduated from MGIMO University with a Ph.D. in economics. He has been in advertising for more than fifteen years, first with Saatchi & Saatchi (Italy and Russia) and then with ADV Group. In October of 2001, he joined McCann Erickson. Holding various positions, he has worked with more than eighty advertisers in Russia, including Procter & Gamble, Nestle, Coca-Cola, Unilever, L'Oreal, Samsung, JTI, Johnson & Johnson, Dirol, and more. He is currently president of Znamenka Creative Agency. He is also vice president of the Social Advertising Creators Association.

Conclusion: How Advertising Really Works

Ron Berger
Chief Executive Officer
Euro RSCG MVBMS Partners
United States

Art or Science?

The question of whether advertising is an art or a science is often debated. The answer is that it's a combination of both. The art lies in the ability to create a beautiful picture or photograph that has a selling proposition in it. The art also lies in the ability to take a strategy and frame it in a photograph or television commercial.

The science, or business, involves all the methodologies marketers use to measure the effectiveness of communications, including sales, of course.

The most basic skill needed to create an advertising campaign is to write copy, design the look of an ad, and get it executed in a magazine, in newspapers, or on television. The essentials in advertising are a combination of common sense and clarity. As someone once said, "Common sense isn't common enough in advertising." You always must remember that the people your ads are talking to are your wife, your kids, and your mother-in-law. So, it's critical to keep the message simple and clear. Too much advertising sounds like marketingese. There are also a few pitfalls to watch out for. Stupidity would be one: stupid ideas, overcomplicated strategies, or self-indulgent executions of advertising that don't show understanding of what a brand is all about, are an enormous waste of time and money.

The difference between advertising and other types of marketing is that advertising allows you to reach many people quickly and to get your message out in the specific way you want. This is different, for example, from public relations where the media messages are unpaid and therefore can be changed or diluted by the reporter writing the story. If you run one commercial on the Super Bowl, a lot of people will know who you are. If it's the right message, if it's interesting and relevant, you'll communicate effectively with your target audience. If it isn't, you'll waste an enormous amount of money. Advertising is very efficient. It can sell everything from cars to hamburgers to presidents of the United States. If you want to run for political office and have a lot of money, by the end of next week many people will know who you are. And by the end of the first Tuesday in November, you will know how many people have liked what you have had to say and "bought" your product.

Success can be measured in many ways, but it's critical that the role of advertising be understood before you can decide on how success will be measured. The bottom line has to be the amount of products you sell. You want the advertising campaign to drive business in a measurable and hopefully profitable way. In some corporate advertising, the role of advertising is to drive the image ratings of a company or its brand, but even that is usually quantifiable. There should be absolute accountability for the money being spent.

To succeed in advertising, you need to have a smart, simple strategy and a clear understanding of your audience. You need to articulate clearly and create and execute an idea that motivates people in ways they never would have imagined being motivated. And then you need to pray that you're right.

Building a Brand

To build a brand from scratch, you need a deep understanding of its core values. What does the brand stand for? What does it believe? Does it have a compelling idea—a reason for being? Hopefully, that reason for being is different from that of its competition. You also need smart people to take the values and attributes of the brand and articulate them in a way that clearly differentiates them in the marketplace. And you need to do that in interesting, fresh ways over a number of years. Volvo's core value, for example, has always been about putting people before cars. That is why Volvo focuses so deeply on safety leadership in building its cars; it also shows concern for the environment and the world as a whole. Volvo's tag line, "For life," captures the company's core values perfectly.

Going from nothing to an established brand doesn't happen quickly, and many lessons can be learned from dot-com companies: It's nearly impossible to build a brand in just a few months. In trying to do so, many dot-coms failed miserably, and many advertising agencies should have known better. They took the money these companies dangled, but branding just doesn't happen that simply. Even the companies with high-visibility commercials failed. You don't start with a Super Bowl commercial. You start with a business idea and a set of values. Those values and attributes must have relevance to the audience with which you want to communicate.

Successful brands all have a clear business and marketing strategy. A brand's tone of voice comes out of that strategy and allows the brand to communicate consistently: It looks and feels constant over several years, even as it continues to grow. For example, Nike has had a clear tone of voice for a number of years, even as it evolves. Consumers recognize that and know Nike stands for a different set of values, human achievement, and not simply for athletic shoes or apparel. This is very different from brands that try to hit "home runs" and breakthrough all the time. The mentality of breaking through has people trying to do things that might be one-shot wonders, like a firework that goes up and crashes down again. There is no shortcut for building a brand that will endure.

The Need to Change

People's lives today are changing in rapid, dramatic ways that we could only dream of a few years ago. The role brands play has to change along with that. To take a brand to the next level, you need to deepen your understanding of the target audience: how their lives and needs are changing. You must continue to develop the product and enhance its attributes so it remains in line with consumers' lives. Smart marketers recognize how people's lifestyles are changing and are constantly looking for ways to make sure their products and communications continue to be relevant. Strong brands can survive forever if they continue to understand and adapt. But to do that, several things must happen. You can never take for granted that what made you successful will continue to make you successful, but you should always know why it made you successful. You need to understand how the marketplace has changed and continue to develop products that deliver on that understanding. This is not to say you should totally reinvent the brand, because that causes confusion. People don't care enough to stay with weak brands or inferior products. They don't have the time to follow brands that keep changing what they are.

The enormous turnover in management is one of the big problems in business today. A new chief executive officer or marketing director comes in, begins questioning what has been done, and changes the marketing focus of the company. That lack of consistency can be very dangerous and damaging to strong brands.

Here is an amazing statistic: Something like 53 percent of the Fortune 500 companies that existed in 1983 aren't around anymore. That's right, more than half of the biggest, most powerful companies in the world just twenty years ago aren't around today. But they have been replaced. Look at how we all live our lives today. We buy our coffee at Starbucks, our clothes at Banana Republic, our books at Amazon. Home Depot, Staples, Circuit City—name a category, and it's likely that a brand that didn't exist fifteen or twenty years ago is dominating our everyday lives. Why? The people who created these brands understood how our lives are changing and developed products, marketing, and advertising that made them an essential part of people's lives.

Just Around the Corner

Technology has brought significant change to the advertising industry. The Internet enables us to do something dramatically different and tremendously important that we otherwise wouldn't have been able to do: to have a two-way conversation with consumers. A television commercial is a one-way conversation—it's the brand talking to the consumer. The Internet allows us to engage in a dialogue with people who are interested in having that conversation. We can ask if you're interested in more information on Product A, and by telling us you are, you're inviting a conversation. That's a tremendously important and valuable tool that wasn't available a few years ago. But it needs to be understood as just a part of the marketing plan. It doesn't replace traditional media, but it is a powerful tool that smart marketers are using more and more.

The role technology plays will continue to drive changes in our industry, because it's going to continue to drive changes in people's lives. What will be developed in terms of mobility and technology will bring to life a way of living and working that, until now, we've only heard and read about. Intel, for example, is introducing a new generation of wireless technology that will allow us to do virtually anything, anywhere: in effect, to unwire our lives. It's not science fiction. This will happen. It will affect all industries. As a result, the way we communicate with people and what we communicate about has to change as well.

In addition to the technology-related changes, the advertising industry has changed its focus. It has become more about the business of advertising than the advertising business. As more agencies have been consolidated into publicly held companies, too much of the discussion has been about a holding company's forecasts, earnings, and profits. It is understandable, but has changed the focus from the quality of the work we do to the quality of the earnings we report. It's a significant shift that began a few years ago. The impact has been that people within the industry—certainly creative people—have lost a little of the magic and also their passion for what advertising can be. It's now about the bottom-line profit more than the craft of what we create. It hasn't affected clients as much: They work for businesses and are accustomed to having to report earnings. Within agencies, it's a more recent phenomenon. Most of the consolidation has happened, so chances are that trend won't accelerate any more than it has in the last few years. Hopefully in the next few years, we will find a happier balance between the quality of the product that agencies deliver to clients and the ability to deliver what shareholders need.

Even with this focus on the bottom line, I think we are living in a tremendously exciting time where, more than ever, clients need what great advertising people have always delivered: big powerful business ideas that can drive businesses in dramatic, profitable ways.

Ron Berger has been in the advertising business since age eighteen when he took the summer job of mail boy and centerfielder for the old Carl Ally agency.

In the thirteen years Mr. Berger worked there, he won hundreds of awards. His most widely acclaimed work, the "Time to Make the Donuts" campaign for Dunkin' Donuts, was honored by the Television Bureau of Advertising as one of the five best commercials of the 1980s.

In 1986, Mr. Berger co-founded the agency that became Messner Vetere Berger McNamee Schmetterer Euro RSCG. The agency was the fastest growing major agency in the advertising industry, boasting a client roster of the world's most forward-thinking companies. As founding partner and chief creative officer, Mr. Berger was involved in some of the most memorable campaigns of the past decade. His commercial for Volvo, entitled "Survivors," was selected "Best Commercial of 1993" by Advertising Age.

In recognition of his work, Mr. Berger was featured in the Wall Street Journal's *Creative Leader campaign.*

Named chief executive officer of MVBMS Euro RSCG in 1999, Mr. Berger continued to lead the agency's innovative approach to advertising. Overseeing a $1.3 billion agency, he also was named chair of the creative committee for the American Association of Advertising Agencies. He sits on the advisory board of the Children's Health Fund and the creative review committee for the Partnership for a Drug-Free America.

Mr. Berger recently completed co-directing and co-producing a feature-length documentary entitled "The Boys of 2nd Street Park," shown at the 2002 Sundance Film Festival and slated to air on Showtime.

With the creation of Euro RSCG MVBMS Partners in 2002, Mr. Berger began the next evolution of his leadership, leading a dynamic new agency that offers Creative Business Ideas™ across all marketing disciplines to a wide array of top brands.

Appendix

CONTENTS

APPENDIX A

AGENCY AGREEMENT # ___

Moscow

_____ 200__

LLC "_____," hereinafter referred to as the Agent, legal entity under the laws of Russia, represented by in the person of General director _____, acting on the basis of the Charter, on the one hand and _____, hereinafter referred to as the Principal, legal entity under the laws of _____, represented by in the person of _____, acting on the basis of _____, on the other hand, hereinafter together or separately referred to as the Parties or the Party accordingly, concluded the present Agency agreement (hereinafter Agreement) as follows:

1. Subject matter of the Agreement

1.1. Present Agreement regulates general principles of relationships of the Parties, their obligations and responsibilities appearing while execution of this Agreement.

1.2. The Agent shall, subject agency remuneration defined in the present Agreement; to perform under the Principal's request legal acts and deeds on the Agent's behalf but at the Principal's expense. Concrete orders of the Principal will be in the form of cost estimates and will be mentioned in the Agent's invoices and Acts of acceptance for each order of the Principal.

2. Obligations of the Parties

2.1. The Agent under the Principal's request concludes contracts with third parties on production of advertising materials, adaptation of materials, dubbing of materials and performance of other actions in according to the Principal's requests.

2.2. While fulfilling Principal's requests, the Agent shall do everything possible to obtain maximum effect and results mutually beneficial to the Parties.

2.3. The Principal, within the framework of this Agreement, undertakes:

2.3.1.To make payments to the Agent necessary to perform the Principal's requests, to provide the Agent with the documents required by the Agent in order to perform its duties arising from this Agreement.

2.3.2. To submit on time information and materials necessary to the Agent to perform its obligations.

2.3.3. To approve on time plans, schedules, materials and also cost estimates, as well as other proposals submitted by the Agent, or inform the Agent in writing about the refusal to approve them within 7 (seven) working days after receiving the above-mentioned documents.

2.3.4. To accept the works performed (or services rendered) under this Agreement or inform the Agent in writing about the refusal to approve them within 7 (seven) working days after the receipt of Acceptance Report from the Agent.

2.3.5. To pay the Agent its remuneration in accordance with the terms and conditions set forth herein.

3. Approvals, authority, amendments

3.1. The Agent shall submit to the Principal for general approval timings, texts, lay-outs and other advertising materials, and also cost estimates on fulfilling Principal's requests.

3.2. The Principal shall approve submitted by the Agent documents referred to in sections 3.1. within 7 (seven) days after receiving the documents. If Principal does not approve the above documents the Parties shall resolve disagreements through negotiations;

3.3. The Principal shall have the right to demand at any time in writing that the Agent amends, suspends or terminates any work or service previously agreed upon, even if by the moment such an instruction is given these works or services have been started already. In this case the Agent will do everything possible to meet this requirement provided that the Agent may act accordingly in compliance with obligations thereof to third parties engaged in execution of these works or services.

The Agent, within 10 (ten) working days, shall inform the Principal of expenses incurred by the Agent or third parties at the moment of following new Principal's instructions. The Principal undertakes to reimburse any expenses already incurred by Agent or third parties by indicated moment and pay remuneration due to the Agent.

3.4. The Agent undertakes to provide Principal with statements of expenses incurred by the Agent upon completion of works or in case of ceasing of present agreement.

4. Cost of the Agent's services, Agency remuneration, order of payments

4.1. Agency remuneration for performance of the Principal's requests is _____ % on net cost (without VAT) of third parties works (services) under the Agent's contracts concluded to fulfill the Principal's requests.

4.2. Cost of third parties works (services) under the Agent's contracts concluded to fulfill the Principal's requests shall be paid by the Principal in following manner:

4.2.1. Against Agent's invoices within 14 (fourteen) working days from the date of the invoice.

4.2.2. Should in according third parties requirements full or partial prepayment is necessary, the Agent shall notify the Principal. In that case the Principal shall within 3 (three) working days communicate to the Agent its consent or refusal of prepayment. In the case of Principal's consent the Principal shall effect prepayment against Agent's invoice before third parties begin executing works (services). In the case of Principal's refusal of prepayment the Agent shall not bear responsibility for delay, termination, stopping or non-performance of any works (services) and also for increasing of works (services) costs, including the Agent shall not reimburse to the Principal all and any losses, connected with Principal's refusal of prepayment.

4.3. Invoices concerning agency remuneration stipulated by p. 4.1. of the present Agreement shall be issued together with invoices mentioned in p. 4.2. of the present Agreement. In situation provided in p. 4.2.2. of the present Agreement the agency remuneration shall be paid after third parties complete works (services) within 14 working days after date of the Agent's invoice.

4.4. Invoices to the Principal will be issued in U.S. dollars. All the payments to be done by the Principal under the Agreement will be effected in U.S. Dollars.

4.5. If the Principal has any objections with regards to the received invoice he should inform the Agent about this within 3 (three) working days from its receipt. Otherwise the invoice is considered accepted.

4.6. The Principal on monthly basis will reimburse the Agent for courier expenses for delivering materials connected with performing by the Agent of its obligations under this Agreement no later than 10 date of the next month against the Agent's invoice with back up documents accompanied. No commissions provided by this Agreement for the Agent will be charged on courier expenses.

5. Confidential Information

5.1. The Agent acknowledges a duty not to disclose without Principal's permission during or after working with the Principal of any confidential information, or any other information resulting out from studies or research commissioned and paid by Principal under this Agreement. The Principal, in turn, acknowledges the Agent's right to use as the Agent sees fit any general marketing or advertising information, which the Agent has gained in the course of Agent's appointment in the field of Principal's product or service.

5.2. The Agent acknowledges its responsibility to treat in complete confidence all the marketing and sales information and statistics which Principal may supply the Agent with.

5.3. Principal undertakes not to disclose and transfer to third parties the concepts, ideas and other materials created by the Agent without the Agent's consent in writing.

6. Copyrights

6.1. The Agent after the Principal have made full payment of the cost of third parties services and Agent remuneration under the present Agreement shall give Principal exclusive rights to use advertising materials (exclusive property rights to the materials including all ways of use mentioned in p.2 art. 16, p.2 art. 37, p. 2 art. 38 of the Russian Law "On copyrights and similar rights"), produced under this Agreement without limitation on time and territory. Transferring of rights should be under the Act of acceptance.

6.2. When possible the Agent shall secure for the Principal any third party copyright or relevant permissions and licenses, with special agreed exception. The Agent shall, in all cases, notify the Principal in writing of any usufructuary restrictions by third parties.

6.3. The Agent undertakes to use advertising material in the Principal's interests. The Agent shall not have the right to use advertising material without prior written permission from the Principal.

7. Liabilities

7.1. In case Parties fail to perform or unduly perform their obligations under the present Agreement Parties shall bear responsibility in accordance with this Agreement and current legislation of the Russian Federation.

7.2. Invoices not paid up by the Principal within stipulated deadlines shall be liable to specific finance charge in the amount of 0.1% (zero point one percent) for each day of delay.

7.3. The Principal shall bear full responsibility for non-compliance of information (quality, violation of the services and goods delivery schedule, etc.) used in the advertising material on Principal's demand to reality and current legislation, as well as for the advertising materials contents. However, the Agent is obliged to inform the Principal about the statutory requirements set forth for such advertising material.

7.4. The Principal shall be responsible for violation of third party's rights (rights to trademark or logo or music, etc.), arising from the Agent using in advertising such materials provided by the Principal. The Agent shall be liable for violation of third party's rights arising from the material provided by the Agent.

7.5. The Agent shall bear no responsibility for the timing of carrying out works or services in case Principal fails to perform its obligations under the present Agreement in due time.

8. Force-majeure

8.1. Parties shall be exempt from responsibility for partial or complete failure to fulfill obligations under the present Agreement in case force-majeure circumstances occur, including:

- acts of God, weather conditions, resulting Parties' inability to carry out obligations under the present Agreement;
- political unrest, riots, military actions and their consequences, which may influence implementing of the obligations under the present Agreement;
- bills issued by authorities and governmental bodies which make it impossible for Parties to carry out their obligations;
- any other circumstances beyond reasonable control of Parties.

8.2. Execution of obligations by Parties shall be postponed for the period of the force-majeure events and their consequences. Parties shall notify their counterpart under this Agreement of the fact that the Party has no opportunity to carry out its obligations under the Agreement in writing within three days of the date of occurrence of the above circumstances.

8.3. In case the above said circumstances last over six months each Party shall have the right to refuse to further carry out its obligations under the present Agreement having notified the other Party of the Agreement cancellation two weeks prior and after all disputes have been resolved. To settle the above issues a commission shall be appointed consisting of equal number of both Parties' representatives.

9. Validity Period of the Agreement

9.1. The present Agreement shall enter into force from the date it has been signed by both Parties and shall be in force until one of the Parties notifies the other Party in writing of this Agreement cancellation at least 60 (sixty) days prior. Supplementary Agreements, Protocols and Enclosures to this Agreement shall enter into force and be terminated accordingly, unless otherwise provided for by these documents.

9.2. By the moment of the Agreement cancellation Principal shall finally settle payments with Agent and pay to Agent all the amounts due.

9.3. In case Principal notifies Agent of cancellation of the present Agreement, Enclosure or Protocol to the Agreement, and Agent by that moment has spent funds on carrying out certain works or services for which Principal gave his consent but the works are not completed by the moment of the above documents' cancellation, Principal shall reimburse Agent's expenses on the basis of documents provided by Agent.

9.4. Liability during the Agreement termination.
Except the case when this Agreement is cancelled as a result of actions causing damage to one of the Parties by the other Party, the rights, liabilities and responsibility of Agent and Principal shall retain in full force during the term of notification.

10. Other Terms

10.1. Any additions, amendments to this Agreement, Protocols and Enclosures thereto shall be made in writing by authorized representatives of Parties.

10.2. Disputes between Parties arising in connection with this Agreement shall be resolved by way of negotiations by authorized representatives of Parties. If Parties fail to reach an agreement the disputes shall be resolved in Moscow Arbitration Court.

10.3. This Agreement is done in two copies, one for each Party, both copies having equal legal force.

10.4. This Agreement is done in Russian and English languages. In case of any disputes the Russian version will prevail.

11. Jurisdiction

11.1. Rights, liabilities and responsibility of Parties under the present Agreement shall be governed by and construed in accordance with the laws of the Russian Federation.

Addresses and bank details

Agent:

Principal:

_____
Acc # _____
Corr. Acc. # _____
In Bank _____

Both parties manifest their agreement to the terms and conditions of this contract by signing below:

Principal   **Agent**

_____   _____

Courtesy of Alexander Mozhaev, Znamenka Creative Agency

International Best Sellers

- **International Patent Law** - A Country-by-Country Look at Patent Laws, Filing Procedures, Contracts, Documents, Litigation, and More - $299.95 (This Book Will be Available June 2004 - Pre-Order Today and Save $50 - Call 1-866-Aspatore to Order)

- **The International M&A Handbook** - A Country-by-Country Look at Doing Deals, Valuations, Legal Documents, and More - $299.95 (This Book Will be Available August 2004 - Pre-Order Today and Save $75 - Call 1-866-Aspatore to Order)

- **Winning Legal Strategies: International Labor & Employment Laws** - A Country-by-Country Look at Labor/Employment Laws, Customs and Holidays, Disputes, Rules, Regulations, Litigation, and More - The Book Also Includes Sample Documents and Contracts Used in the Biggest International Countries - $299.95 (This Book Will be Available September 2004 - Pre-Order Today and Save $100 - Call 1-866-Aspatore to Order)

- **International Product Liability Law** - A Worldwide Desk Reference Featuring Laws and Customs in Over Fifty Countries - $219.95

- **The Global Venture Capital Handbook** - A Country-by-Country Look Featuring Local Venture Capitalists on What it Takes to Succeed (From an Investment and Entrepreneurial Standpoint) in Their Region and Important Country Laws, Statistics, and Other Valuable Information - $219.95

- **International Software Distribution & Agreements** - A Country-by-Country Look Featuring Leading Executives and Lawyers on What it Takes to Profit in Their Region and Important Country Laws, Statistics, and Other Valuable Information - $219.95 (This Book Will be Available July 2004 - Pre-Order Today and Save $75 - Call 1-866-Aspatore to Order)

- **Outsourcing Agreements Line by Line** - Leading Outsourcing Lawyer Joe Rosenbaum on Making it Fit Your Needs - Includes Detailed Analysis of Actual Outsourcing Contract - $149.95 (This Book Will be Available September 2004 - Pre-Order Today and Save $50 - Call 1-866-Aspatore to Order)

- **Outsourcing to India** - An Executive Overview on Outsourcing Best Suited to India, Benefits, Compensation in India, Country Resources, and More - $149.95 (This Book Will be Available September 2004 - Pre-Order Today and Save $50 - Call 1-866-Aspatore to Order)

- **Being There Without Going There** - Managing Teams Across Time Zones, Locations, and Corporate Boundaries - $24.95

- **International Advertising Best Practices** - A Country-by-Country Look at Ad Strategies, Buying Media, Demographics, Costs and Statistics, and More - $219.95 (This Book Will be Available October 2004 - Pre-Order Today and Save $75 - Call 1-866-Aspatore to Order)

- **The Business Translator** - Business Words, Customs, and Phrases in Over Sixty Languages - $29.95

Legal Best Sellers

Visit Your Local Bookseller Today or Go to www.Aspatore.com For More Information

- International Product Liability Law: A Worldwide Desk Reference Featuring Product Liability Laws and Procedures for Over Fifty Countries - $219
- Winning Antitrust Strategies - Antitrust Chairs from Latham & Watkins, Wachtell, Lipton, and More on the Laws that Regulate, Promote, and Protect Competition - $79.95
- The Art & Science of Patent Law - Patent Chairs from Vinson & Elkins, Foley Hoag, and More on the Laws That Regulate, Promote, and Protect Competition - $37.95
- Inside the Minds: The Art & Science of Bankruptcy Law - Bankruptcy Chairs from Perkins Coie, Reed Smith, Ropes & Grey, and More on Successful Strategies for Bankruptcy Proceedings - $37.95
- Inside the Minds: The Corporate Lawyer - Corporate Chairs From Dewey Ballantine, Holland & Knight, Wolf Block, and More on Successful Strategies for Business Law - $37.95
- Inside the Minds: Firm Leadership - Partners From Dykema Gossett, Thatcher Proffitt & Wood, and More on the Art and Science of Managing a Law Firm - $37.95
- Inside the Minds: The Innovative Lawyer - Managing Partners From Bryan Cave, Jenner & Block, Buchanan Ingersoll, and More on Becoming a Senior Partner in Your Firm - $37.95
- The Art & Science of Antitrust Law - Antitrust Chairs from Proskauer Rose, Weil Gotshal & Manges, Wilson Sonsini, and More on Antitrust, Trade Regulation, and White Collar Defense - $37.95
- Inside the Minds: Leading Deal Makers - Leading Venture Capitalists and Lawyers Share Their Knowledge on Negotiations, Leveraging Your Position, and Deal Making - $37.95
- Inside the Minds: Leading Intellectual Property Lawyers - IP Chairs From Foley & Lardner, Blank Rome, Hogan & Hartson, and More on the Art and Science of Intellectual Property Law - $37.95
- Inside the Minds: Leading Labor Lawyers - Labor/Employment Chairs From Thelen Reid & Pries, Wilson Sonsini, Perkins Coie, and More on the Art and Science of Labor and Employment Law - $37.95
- Inside the Minds: Leading Lawyers - Managing Partners From Akin Gump, King & Spaulding, Morrison & Foerster, and More on the Art and Science of Being a Successful Lawyer - $37.95
- Inside the Minds: Leading Litigators - Litigation Chairs From Weil Gotshal & Manges, Jones Day, and More on the Art and Science of Litigation - $37.95
- Inside the Minds: Leading Product Liability Lawyers - Product Liability Chairs From Debevoise & Plimpton, Kaye Scholer, Bryan Cave, and More on the Art and Science Behind a Successful Product Liability Practice - $37.95
- Inside the Minds: Privacy Matters - Privacy Chairs From McGuireWoods, Kaye Scholer, and More on the Privacy Strategies and the Laws that Govern Privacy - $27.95

**Buy All 14 Books (Excluding International Product Liability Law) and
Save 40% (the Equivalent of Getting 4 Books for Free) - $339.95**

-Or-

**Buy All 15 Books INCLUDING International Product Liability Law and
Save 50% (the Equivalent of Getting 6 Books for Free) - $419.95**

Other Best Sellers

- Ninety-Six and Too Busy to Die - Life Beyond the Age of Dying - $24.95

- Technology Blueprints - Strategies for Optimizing and Aligning Technology Strategy and Business - $69.95

- The CEO's Guide to Information Availability - Why Keeping People and Information Connected is Every Leader's New Priority - $27.95

- Being There Without Going There - Managing Teams Across Time Zones, Locations, and Corporate Boundaries - $24.95

- Profitable Customer Relationships - CEOs from Leading Software Companies on using Technology to Maximize Acquisition, Retention, and Loyalty - $27.95

- The Entrepreneurial Problem Solver - Leading CEOs on How to Think Like an Entrepreneur and Solve Any Problem for Your Team/Company - $27.95

- The Philanthropic Executive - Establishing a Charitable Plan for Individuals and Businesses - $27.95

- The Golf Course Locator for Business Professionals - Organized by Closest to Largest 500 Companies, Cities, and Airports - $12.95

- Living Longer Working Stronger - Seven Steps to Capitalizing on Better Health - $14.95

- Business Travel Bible - Must-Have Phone Numbers, Business Resources, Maps, and Emergency Info - $19.95

- ExecRecs - Executive Recommendations for the Best Business Products and Services Professionals Use to Excel - $14.95

Call 1-866-Aspatore or Visit www.Aspatore.com to Order

ASPATORE
BOOKS